A HISTORY OF
WEBHEATH

Foxlydiate Lane.

A HISTORY OF
WEBHEATH

ELIZABETH ATKINS

BREWIN BOOKS

First published in Great Britain
by Elizabeth Atkins, 2009.

This revised edition published by Brewin Books, 2020.

BREWIN BOOKS
19 Enfield Ind. Estate,
Redditch,
Worcestershire,
B97 6BY
www.brewinbooks.com

A CIP catalogue record for this book is available from the British Library.

Front cover top: St. Philip's, Webheath, c.2000.
Front cover bottom: Meet at Foxlydiate, 1908 (colourised by A. Brewin).
Rear cover: Foxlydiate Lane, c.1900.

ISBN: 978-1-85858-710-3

Printed and bound in Great Britain
by 4edge Ltd.

Contents

List of Illustrations

Acknowledgements

I would like to record my grateful thanks to Chris our son and also my friend Margaret Cockburn, who very kindly and with great patience read and corrected my work. Any mistakes there are, are mine.

I would also like to say thank you to all those local residents who have given me so much information on the locality. In particular: Ruby Gardner, David Thomas, Derek Waugh, Mavis Bristow, Les Bryan, Christine Finney, Ron Tongue, Fred Shrimpton, Barbara Radbourne and many others too numerous to mention.

The diagram on p.11 has been adapted from work carried out by Mr. Steadman, Dept. of Geography, University of Birmingham. WRO Photographic Survey. Every effort has been made to locate the original donors for their permission to use the photos.

A Thousand Years in Tardebigge by Monica Dickens, contains a wealth of information on the parish of Tardebigge. I and many others have benefited from all her research which must have been carried out over a number of years.

Monica Dickens was one of the daughters of Canon Charles Allen Dickens, who was Vicar of Tardebigge for sixty years. He resigned his living in 1915 at the age of eighty-six years and died peacefully the following year.

Elizabeth Atkins

Chapter 1

History of Webheath

Webheath – the name conjures up all sorts of unusual suggestions as to its possible origins, but the real meaning is far more prosaic. As far as we know, the name Webheath first appears in written documents in the early fifteenth century, when it was usually referred to as Webheath and Cur Lane. Both names have had many different spellings which have changed over time, and both places were divisions of the parish of Tardebigge. Cur Lane, Crullelane, Corlond or Curlane,[1] could possibly be a derivation of '*Crowle*' Lane, an Anglo-Saxon word meaning 'bend'. While Webheath has variously been spelt as Wibheath (seventeenth century) or, even earlier in 1481, as Strech Bentley next Wybbeheath,[2] Cur Lane seems to have included part of what was the old parish of Webheath, as both are mentioned in 1650 when there was a levy for Wibheath and Cur Lane. Strech Bentley took its name from the Strech family who lived here in the thirteenth century and appears to be part of the old parish of Webheath, some of Upper Bentley and a field called Coxhiron.[3] The reason why Webheath does not appear in very early documents is because it was just common or waste land.

In the early days only part of the parish of Tardebigge was in the Royal Forest of Feckenham, but Henry II (1154-1189) added a great deal of ground to the forest, which included the site of Bordesley Abbey and all the land in Tardebigge parish east of the road from Bromsgrove to Alcester.[4]

---

1 Monica Dickens p.6.
2 Ibid. p.34.
3 Op. cit. p.34.
4 Op. cit. p.7.

Tardebigge in the Forest of Feckenham

Forests in general and Feckenham in particular, were large tracts of land designated by the Normans in the eleventh and twelfth centuries as areas for hunting – although Royal Forests existed as entities long before England was invaded by the Normans. What the Normans **did** do was to introduce a new concept of the Royal Forest, which profoundly affected the status of the wooded areas in England and the lives of Englishmen for centuries. The key to understanding this concept of the Royal Forest in Medieval England was the King's love of hunting, and it was to protect and conserve the red deer for the King's sport, which was the impetus behind the forest laws introduced by the Normans. The term 'forest', applying to any large, wooded area is relatively recent in origin. The term 'forest', when related to the large tracts of land designated as areas for hunting, had open spaces, cultivated fields and villages and settlements within them. For those who lived within their boundaries, these laws imposed brutal penalties on those who poached animals in the Royal Forest. They placed restrictions on the use of wood in the forest and the clearing of areas in the forest, called assarts, as the King also obtained revenue from Royal Forests. Because the Royal Forest was based on the King's desire to protect areas where the hunting was most favourable, the areas within the Royal Forests coincided roughly with the more heavily wooded areas of England, the same areas that, from a geographical point of view, might also be called forests. Feckenham Forest, together with Wyre Forest, Ombersley and Kinver Forest covered most of Worcestershire. In fact Worcestershire, at one point, was probably the most wooded county in England.

The word 'forest', used in this sense, is strictly a legal term. It meant that the King, or whoever he appointed as the lessee, had the right to hunt over this piece of land and no-one else could kill the beasts of the forest; the red deer, the fallow deer, roe deer and wild boar. As well as these, there were the beasts of the warren, which were the fox, rabbit, hare and badger. Of course, people did poach and it was always those people who were most in need who got caught. The gentry, as well as the local clergy like the Bishop of Worcester, were just as guilty, but they were usually let off with a fine – in other words it was a way of raising money. These people were tried in the great forest courts called Eyres, one of which was held in the Court House which was situated on what is now the football pitch at the back of the village square in Feckenham. All that remains now is a raised area surrounded by two ditches and the site was also almost certainly the site of the King's hunting lodge, which was demolished in 1356.

Those inhabitants cultivating land within a Royal Forest had very stringent laws to follow; they could not stop the protected animals from straying over their land nor could they build ditches or hedges too high so as to stop them. Fences might not be too high so as to impede the deer getting in or out, and a thousand years ago wolves were hunted in the forest. Within the bounds of the forest there were private woods, and parks, two of which were at what is now known as Holyoakes Farm and at Bentley,

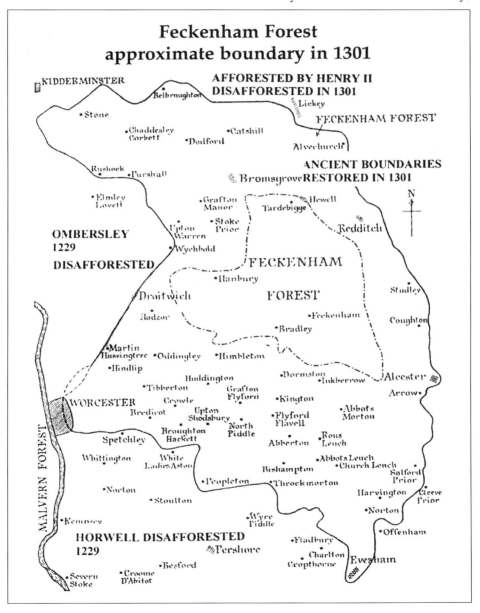

Feckenham Forest
approximate boundary in 1301

KIDDERMINSTER

Belbroughton

Lickey

AFFORESTED BY HENRY II
DISAFFORESTED IN 1301

FECKENHAM FOREST

• Stone

• Chaddesley
Corbett

• Catshill

• Dodford

Alvechurch

Rushock • Purshall

ANCIENT BOUNDARIES
RESTORED IN 1301

Bromsgrove

• Elmley
Lovett

• Grafton
Manor

Tardebigge

Hewell

N

• Stoke
Prior

Redditch

OMBERSLEY
1229

Upton
Warren

DISAFFORESTED

Wychbold

FECKENHAM

• Hanbury

Droitwich

FOREST

Studley

Hadzor

• Feckenham

Coughton

• Bradley

• Martin
Hussingtree

• Oddingley

• Himbleton

• Hindlip

Huddington

Grafton
Flyford

• Tibberton

• Dormston

• Inkberrow

Alcester

Arrow •

WORCESTER

Crowle

• Kington

Bredicot

Upton
Snodsbury

• Flyford
Flavell

• Abbots
Morton

Broughton
Hackett

North
Piddle

Rous
Lench

Spetchley

Abberton

Whittington

White
Ladies Aston

Bishampton

• Abbots Lench
• Church Lench

Salford
Prior

• Norton

• Peopleton

• Throckmorton

Harvington

Cleeve
Prior

• Stoulton

• Norton

Wyre
Piddle

• Offenham

MALVERN FOREST

Kempsey

HORWELL DISAFFORESTED
1229

Pershore

• Fladbury

• Charlton
Cropthorne

Evesham

• Besford

• Severn
Stoke

• Croome
D'Abitot

where Grimbauld Pauncefote had a warren for rabbits. Grimbauld was a powerful forester who was responsible for the maintenance of the forest laws in the area.

Feckenham Forest, at its widest extent, went as far north as The Lickeys and south as far as Evesham on the Worcestershire border. The map on p.3 shows us which places were in existence in the forest at the time of Domesday, as well as those mentioned in 1301. Many of the names are connected with forest areas. For example Foxlydiate, which was originally Fox le hunting gate. Many of the local names like Bentley, which end in 'ley' suggest a clearing in a forest area, since the suffix 'ley' means open space or clearing. The term 'green' is a medieval one, which also means a clearing made in a wooded area. Local examples including Broad Green, Banks Green, Stock Green, Bradley Green, Fosters Green, Grinsty etc. are all remains of clearings made in the forest, for which the landholder would have to pay a fine or fee to the King. Other reminders of the past history of the forest are incorporated into farm names like Forest Farm, Great Lodge Farm and nearby Huntingdrop Farm and Monks Wood. The names of Blickley (which is on the road to Hanbury near Ditchford Bank) and Hollowfields (on the Hanbury/Feckenham road) are all that remains as reminders of deserted medieval villages which existed in the forest. By the mid-thirteenth century the forest was divided into six bailiwicks (a word describing an area under jurisdiction) and the park, each under an hereditary Forester-in-Fee.

These foresters were a law unto themselves. The records of the events chronicled in the accounts of the administration of the forest, and what happened to those people living within the forest limits, makes fascinating reading. They list those who killed various animals and the fines they had to pay, if peasants made clearings (assarts) in the forest bounds, the state of the woods and, in particular, the records show the continued tensions between the local people and the foresters over the customary rights to hospitality claimed by the latter. The records state that the Abbot of Bordesley was expected to provide food and shelter one day a week at a place called *Knottenhull* (in Dodderhill) and for another day of the week at the manor house in Bentley, belonging to Grimbauld Pauncefote. The Rector of Hanbury was also expected to provide hospitality. The Abbot of Bordesley was also expected to look after the foresters in his manor of *Sheltwood*, and the foresters of Walkwood were expected to be looked after at *Tyneshale* (in Tardebigge). The foresters at Lickey saw it as their right to be entertained at the house of the Lord of Catshill, and another at the Grange of the Prior of Dodford.[5] The office of Foresters remained

5 WHS Records of Feckenham Forest Worcestershire c.1236-1377 p.171.

in the same families' hands throughout twelfth and thirteenth centuries.[6] The Bailia of Bentley was in the hands of the Strech family who, as already mentioned, gave their name to Strech Bentley. One of the forest areas was that known as the Bailia de Werkwood (Walkwood). The office of Chief Forester-in-Fee or Warden belonged to another branch of the Strech family; the Astwood Streches.[7] In 1250, Robert Strech held the office.[8] Walkwood, now developed into modern housing estates round what was Walkwood Farm, then extended much further, from Evesham up as far as Bordesley. The extents of the six foresters-in-fees define the total extent of the forest which is, in fact, identical with the perambulation of Edward I (1300-1301). When this perambulation of the forest was confirmed in 1300, it shaped the destinies of the forest and its inhabitants for 300 years. Before that date, the force of forest law had been an important and accepted feature of everyday life and Feckenham, although not the largest of the royal forests, assumed an important place in the royal interest. From 1300 it was reduced to almost insignificant dimensions and a corresponding dwindling of interest in its laws and administrations was the result. The subsequent result was widespread cultivation.[9]

In consequence, the area of Feckenham Forest was reduced to some 34 square miles. Instead of Worcester marking the westernmost extension of the forest, the furthest point was Shell, near Himbleton. In the north instead of Belbroughton, it was Tardebigge. On the east it was The Ridgeway, not the River Arrow and in the south, not Evesham but the hamlets of Stock and Bradley.[10] In some places, the forest boundary was only two miles from the headquarters at Feckenham.

In the thirteenth century when much of the land was heath, moor and woodland, surnames were just beginning to appear and many people adopted the name of the village or place where they lived. In the Lay Subsidy Roll for Tardebigge of 1276 (a list of people paying taxes), one gets names such as Johanne atte Hethe (John by the Heath); Johanne atte Gate (John by the Gate); or Nicholas atte Frith (Nicholas by the Thrift – wood). One also gets William of Shurnock. At Shurnock (which means bright and shining oak), there is a marvellous example of one of the many moated sites in the forest. There are at least ten moated sites in the old parish of Feckenham alone, while in the parish of Tardebigge, there is one at Bentley Pauncefoot. Bentley Pauncefote (Pauncefoot) is a local example in which the role of

6 J. West p.79.
7 Ibid. p.125.
8 Op. cit. p.125.
9 J. West p.83.
10 WHS 1960 Miscellany I. pp.37/8.

names is reversed, where the person's name (Grimbauld Pauncefote, whose name means 'arched belly'), has been attached to the original Anglo-Saxon term, to become Bentley Pauncefote (now Pauncefoot). He and his brothers were always poaching the King's deer, as well as being part of the lesser gentry who lived in the forest.[11] Another Pauncefote – Isabella – was just as bad. In one incident two known offenders called Richard Marshall and Robert Strech came upon some poachers and captured one of their hunting dogs which they took to the home of William Marshall, one of the keepers. The next night, a band of men from Isabella's family broke into the house, retrieved the dog by force and removed it to the house at Bentley.[12] The Pauncefote family also had the right to build a rabbit warren in the forest, enclosing it with a ditch and a low hedge. There used to be a field in Bentley called Coneygreen; 'coney' is another word for rabbit, but all evidence of the rabbit warren has disappeared after years of cultivation. It is believed that the moated site (which is on private property), is all that remains of the Pauncefote house, or at least near the site of the original manor house. The clue to the location might be in the name of the moated site, which was called the Banqueting Orchard.[13]

The reasons for moats are many and have changed over time. Originally defensive, they evolved to provide shelter for the people and animals within the moat. Later they were used as status symbols. At one point Shurnock, on the Droitwich/Alcester Road, had a drawbridge over the moat. During the civil war the Edgioke family occupied it. They were supporters of Parliament and the house suffered at the hands of the cavaliers. After which, it was handed back to the Bishop of Worcester.

One interesting point is, that while most of the forests were the definite property of the crown, sometimes the King alienated (bestowed) some of them to his subjects. But, although a King or a subject may have had all the rights in the forest, he may not necessarily have held all the land which it comprised; as was the case in the Forest of Feckenham. Other persons may have possessed lands within the bounds of a forest but were not allowed the right of hunting or of cutting trees in them without permission.

The Administration of the forest was built in tiers. At the top was the **Keeper**, a very important person, usually a lord, who took the title and all the perks that went with it. Geoffrey Chaucer was one such person – although it is not recorded whether he actually visited Feckenham. Under The Keeper were the **Chief Foresters**, each of whom had the responsibility

---

11 WHS Records of Feckenham Forest Worcestershire c.1236-1377 p.148.
12 Ibid. p.68.
13 WRO Tithe Award Map Tardebigge 1838.

for the bailiwicks or different areas and at the beginning were a law unto themselves. One of these was named Richard Toki whose name lives on in the farm name Tookey's Farm at Astwood Bank. Another Forester was Robert Strech of Strech Bentley as well as Richard de Benetleg.[14] In these bailiwicks one would also have a **Woodward** who was directly responsible to the King as he was responsible for the protection of the private woods. People were allowed to take brushwood, but building timber presented a greater problem. The question of the availability of timber presented the simplest and most obvious test of how much living in a royal forest posed a hardship, because villeins were held responsible for their own buildings, only the miller's building was the lord's responsibility. Removal of timber was an offence and the same court which ordered repairs of dilapidated buildings as frequently punished tenants for their repair.

After 1301, many of these offices disappeared when the outer limits of the forest were dis-afforested or taken out of the royal forest. In the fifteenth and sixteenth centuries new offices appeared; that of Steward, Ranger, Master of the Game and Rider or Parker, which were given away as perks to local landowners.

It was obvious by then that the importance of the forest was decreasing. Finally, by decree in 1629, the forest ceased to be a Royal Forest. The decree was finalised in 1632 and the land was then sold off; first to Edward Leighton the then Lord of the Manor, who subsequently sold it to Thomas Lord Coventry, who became Lord of the Manor of Feckenham. The present Lord Coventry is still Lord of the Manor.

After its removal from the administration of the forest, it is clear from archaeological evidence that the land in Webheath and Tardebigge continued to be occupied and cultivated, from evidence of ridge and furrow (which still exists), showing the continual ploughing of the land. This ridge and furrow shows the evidence of earlier field boundaries. The scarcity of trees and root holes suggests that the land was already open land in the medieval period, perhaps being used for grazing. Some evidence of this ridge and furrow can still be seen in the field on the right hand side below Holly Cottage in Church Road.[15] (See photograph on p.8)

Early Webheath

The boundaries of the parish covered a far greater area in the past. They extended as far as Sheltwood Farm, down through part of Upper Bentley, across Crumpfields and Heathfield Road, along Birchfield Road

14 WHS Vol.21 Records of Feckenham Forest 1236-1377. p.12.
15 Arch. Report. 1997.

to Headless Cross and back along the other side of the road including Tack Farm, the outskirts of Hewell Grange and up to Tardebigge Church. (See map on inside cover)

Webbheath or Wybbe Heath, as it appears to have been named hundreds of years ago, probably took its name from a family called Wybb who lived in this part of the world around the 1200s. Curlane, mentioned in old documents, was usually referred to with Webheath. The name still exists in the modern description of the lane which leads from what was Boxnott Farm, through towards Stoke Pound passing on the way a farm now called Tardebigge Farm, but in times gone by was referred to as Webbs Farm or House. The old lane used to turn up into what is now Holyoakes Lane (or Gypsy Lane), to finish up at the church. From a description of the lands which made up Cur Lane, it suggests that Cur Lane must have been an area of land between the modern day Webheath and Tardebigge Church, but a more careful study needs to be done.

Some of the land in Webheath called Tynsalle field, was the ground between the Alcester/Bromsgrove Road and Holyoakes Lane,[16] which was originally part of the land belonging to the Abbey at Bordesley. When

Picture of ridge and furrow, Church Road, Webheath.

---

16 MD op. cit. p.27.

the monasteries were suppressed by Henry VIII, the land belonging to the Abbey was sold by the crown to Lord *Wyndsor* in 1542,[17] including the lordship of Strech Bentley, hence Lord Windsor became Lord of the Manor of Tardebigge. When the properties belonging to Lord Windsor (who by then had been created the Earl of Plymouth in 1905) were sold off in c.1947 to meet death duties, the Lordship of the Manor was also sold – to Alderman Howard Bird.

Before we had county courts, much of the day to day business of the manor would have been carried out at the court leet or court baron, held by the steward of the manor on behalf of the Lord of the Manor, in this case Lord Windsor. At the meetings of the manorial courts, reeves, constables and ale tasters were appointed to make sure that everything in the parish was run smoothly; if people transgressed then they were fined. At one of these courts six people were presented for keeping ale houses and refusing to sell ale by the approved measure.[18] Bakers were fined if they did not weigh their bread to conform to the statutory weights and measures and butchers for killing calves if they were less than five weeks old. The Court Rolls (the official records of the manor) are full of interesting references to the people of the locality. Humfrey Stafford of Grafton is mentioned in 1481, when he came to the court to sell some land which he held round the present Tack Farm cottages at Foxlydiate (now Harbours Hill),[19] while his father, also Sir Humfrey, continued to hold land in Tardebigge. Four years later, Sir Humfrey fought for Richard III at the battle of Bosworth. He obtained a pardon from Henry VII, but was later taken and executed and his property including his land in Tardebigge was confiscated.[20]

In Elizabethan times there were two constables for the whole manor and five headboroughs including two for Wibheath and Curlane. The ale tasters probably had a lot to do as there were no licensing laws; the manorial courts were the sole authority for all administrative and other minor local offences. In 1596 a man named Dudatus Perks was Headborough for Wibbheath, until he and his wife, were buried in 1613.[21] Another local inhabitant who played a part in the administration of the parish was William Callow, who was Constable for Webheath and Cur Lane in 1720. Lanehouse Lane was at one point known as Hemlock Lane and it is described as the lane leading from Webheath to Tardebigge Church.[22] Lanehouse Lane was

---

17 MD op. cit. p.34/5.
18 MD op. cit. p.48.
19 MD op. cit. p.46.
20 MD op. cit. p.52.
21 MD op. cit. p.92.
22 MD op. cit. p.92.

part of William Callow's copyhold property and in 1771 he was one of the landowners concerned with the enclosure of Webheath.

The large amount of unenclosed land in the parish meant that people were tempted to encroach, in other words build on waste land, very often at the side of roads. These people then paid a fine to the Lord of the Manor and were allowed to carry on living there. You can see an example of this very clearly from the position of the thatched cottage in Foxlydiate Lane, which must have been built on what was the waste land by the side of the lane.

The commons or wastes of the seventeenth century, were Redditch, Lynenwood (which went from Redditch to the Alcester Road at Foxlydiate), and Wibheath (from Webheath Lane to Foxlydiate). This area roughly approximates to the land surrounded by Heathfield Road, Birchfield Road, Foxlydiate Lane and what is now known as Church Road. Bentley Heath covered the area near what is now Cur Lane and Banks Green and Coxhiron, from the other side of Cur Lane to the Holyoaks.[23] Heathfield and Birchfield are self explanatory, although Heathfield Road was originally called Webheath Lane. Church Road was not named as such until the church was built in 1870. It may have been called previously Foxlydiate Road (1851 Census) or Curlane, or more probably just Hill Top. Place and road names have never been static but have evolved over time, so it is sometimes difficult to chart their changes and whereabouts.

In the seventeenth century the Feckenham side of what is now Heathfield Road is shown on Blagrave's map of the Forest and Manor of Feckenham, originally drawn in 1591 and copied in 1744 by John Doherty the Younger. Shown as fields, they were on the edge of what was described as Wybbheath. The land had already been taken out of the wooded area known then as Red Slow Coppice and parcelled up into separate fields, occupied by quite a few householders. There is a property shown on the corner of Botters Hill (now Green Lane), where Sycamore Farm is situated. The property belonged to Humphrey Jennets, the landholder at Norgrove, who had an under-tenant. Continuing along, there were five further plots with houses situated on them, probably half-timbered; all were under-tenants of Henry Bolte, a prosperous yeoman farmer who lived at Lower Grinsty Farmhouse. Lower Grinsty is situated in the middle of what is now Redditch Golf Club. By the end of the nineteenth century all this land was part of the Sillins Estate, which belonged to the Haywood family; the little properties had disappeared, and some of the land had already been developed.

---

23 MD op. cit. p.54.

The Eighteenth Century

Even up to the eighteenth century much of the land was not enclosed. The wide open fields were divided into different plots and farmed by various tenants/owners. In the late eighteenth century these fields, commons and wastes were divided up and enclosed with hedges and ditches and allotted to various landowners. If one looks at old maps of Webheath, one can see very clearly the regular shape of the fields which had been divided up out of the waste land. Of course this is the land which has now been built on,

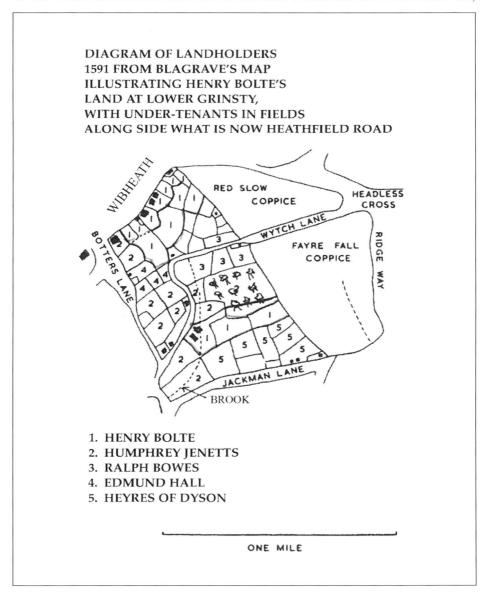

DIAGRAM OF LANDHOLDERS
1591 FROM BLAGRAVE'S MAP
ILLUSTRATING HENRY BOLTE'S
LAND AT LOWER GRINSTY,
WITH UNDER-TENANTS IN FIELDS
ALONG SIDE WHAT IS NOW HEATHFIELD ROAD

1. HENRY BOLTE
2. HUMPHREY JENETTS
3. RALPH BOWES
4. EDMUND HALL
5. HEYRES OF DYSON

ONE MILE

much of which in the last twenty years. These fields would have been sown with cereals of various sorts as well as being used for pasture. As well as sugar beet being grown at one period, there are allusions to the growing of flax or hemp at Foxlydiate.[24]

Webheath was described as being an area 2,185 acres of which 438 acres were arable and the rest permanent grassland. This is explained by the composition of its soil, which is stiff loam with a subsoil of Keuper marl.[25] Until the early 1800s Webheath had a mainly rural economy. The common land was enclosed in 1771, and if one looks at the Tithe Apportionment Map of 1838, the original common land can be seen very clearly with its regular shaped fields in the area between what is now Heathfield Road and Foxlydiate Lane. Until the 1940s, the conterminous ecclesiastical parish boundaries of Tardebigge and the old parish of Feckenham ran down the middle of Heathfield Road. Family historians find it very difficult to identify where their relatives might have lived, especially when looking at census returns because they may state that they were born in Tardebigge – meaning the Tardebigge side of Webheath Lane or Feckenham meaning the Feckenham side of the lane.

Debates have often taken place over the precise lines of the boundaries of parishes both civil and ecclesiastical, as well as county boundaries. As is known Tardebigge and Feckenham lie on the county boundaries of Worcestershire and Warwickshire. At one point the county boundary ran right through the middle of Tardebigge Church and the boundary dispute was not settled until the nineteenth century.[26] The Ridgeway was traditionally the county boundary between Worcestershire and Warwickshire, but, in the 1930s the boundary ran behind the properties at Headless Cross and went down The Mayfields to Upper Ipsley and continued across to Gorcott Hill.

During the first half of the eighteenth century the need for improving means of transport was, each year, becoming more urgent. Local industries developed, making improvements to the roads even more necessary. As in other counties, rural parishes complained because they had to maintain the local roads even though they were used by 'foreigners'. The overseer for this job was the Surveyor of the Highways, who was unpaid and appointed from among the parishioners. He was obliged to survey the highways three times a year and organise labour that was provided by

---

24 Ibid. p.83.
25 VCH Worcestershire Vol.III p.223.
26 Ibid. p.223.

landholders to repair the roads.[27] It was not until the late seventeenth century that parliament granted powers to collect tolls on certain roads and also authorised the setting up of obstructions to prevent people using them without paying by the erection of a 'turnpike' or gate.

One of the earliest road maps is that drawn by John Ogilby (1600-1676). He introduced road or coaching maps, showing the roads in strip form with an accompanying description. In his map of the road from Hereford to Leicester, he describes the section which ran through Droitwich to Bromsgrove and then Burcot (spelt Burcoate) through to Alvechurch as 'an indifferent straight way which leads to Alchurch'. The map itself shows turnings off it to the right to Hewell Grange, so one can only guess what condition the little side roads would have been in.

Numerous Acts from 1706 onwards allowed the creation of Turnpike Trusts; lengths of roads were withdrawn from parish control and placed under the management of appointed persons with authority to collect tolls for the maintenance of roads. Monica Dickens in her book *A Thousand Years in Tardebigge*, gives a good description of the roads in the parish,

'In 1754 there was an Act for repairing and widening the roads… through Hewell Lane and Burcot to the Cross of Hands on a common called the Lickhay: and out of Hewell Lane through Church Lane and Tutnell to Bromsgrove. (At that time the road from the Hewell Lodges to New Wharf did not exist.) The roads of that day were so different from those of today that it is difficult to get a true idea of them. Many of them quite unfenced only on the east side in 1675. That this condition was usual is suggested by a Turnpike Law of 1763, which forbids any person to make any hedge, ditch or fence on any turnpike road not enclosed on both sides nor to plough or harrow, or turn the plough or harrow within the distance of fifteen feet from the centre of any turnpike road.'[28]

Tolls were determined by the type of traffic using the roads. There were three turnpikes or tollbars in Tardebigge. The Hewell Lane gate stood at the top of the hill by the allotments, the house being on the park side of the road. Hewell Lane was marked on a map as a mail road in 1825. At Tutnall the gate crossed the Bromsgrove Road. Monica Dickens comments that the house was still there c.1930. This gate caught the traffic between

27 Gaut p.115.
28 MD op. cit. p.95.

Bromsgrove and Redditch which up to the nineteenth century travelled up the Holloway to Broad Green and thence via Brockhill. The third tollbar stood just below the entrance to New Wharf but was not in existence until c.1831.[29]

Hewell Lane as 'a mail road' was part of the four coach roads from London to Holyhead. The coach must have been an amazing sight as it flashed through Tardebigge at about seven o'clock each morning and evening. In 1787 it was a new thing to have a post every day. On this mail road ran the 'London Waggon' and on it the passengers must have had many adventures. By 1823 there were two coach roads running through Tardebigge parish. One, already mentioned, running along Hewell Lane, the Ridgeway to Headless Cross and the other through Redditch to Birmingham.

The Poor

Poor people caused endless trouble to parish authorities upon whom fell the responsibility of looking after their own paupers, as they were described.[30] Who were the deserving poor? It was most difficult to decide, but a law was passed in 1662 which defined the poor, among which; those who needed assistance, as well as those people who had lived in a parish for forty days. They should be deemed as belonging to it, or as it was termed gain settlement to it; but that, within that time a stranger could be sent back to the village from whence they had come. Other Acts were passed which enabled the poor to move from one parish to another if they had a 'certificate'. A poor rate was set by the local JPs and contributed to by the local ratepayers.

Overseers of the Poor were selected by 'the vestry' to levy a poor rate and supervise its distribution. Young people were set as apprentices into local work while the sick and the elderly whose claims were allowed, were sometimes given a small pension, although after 1697 they had to wear a large 'P' on their outer garments. Tardebigge agricultural labourers may have received a similar amount as those in Inkberrow, which was from 6s. to 7s. per week with food, or 9s. to provide for themselves.[31] In 1723 a general Act allowed parishes to build and erect workhouses or houses of industry, although not every parish in the immediate vicinity built them straight away. For example Feckenham's House of Industry was built in 1796, and Alcester's in 1774. It is not clear when the workhouse for Tardebigge, Redditch and Webheath was built. A workhouse is listed in

---

29 Ibid. p.96.
30 Gaut p.103.
31 Eden p.348.

the Rent Rolls for the Plymouth estate in 1770,[32] but it is not clear whether it is the one which was situated in Pumphouse Lane and is now known as Pumphouse Farm. Pumphouse Farm was closed as a workhouse c.1834 when the Poor Law Act formed parishes into 'Unions' and the parish of Tardebigge was incorporated into the Bromsgrove Union. The workhouse for the Union was situated in the Birmingham Road, now called Bartleet House, while the 'Union' for Feckenham was the Alcester Union. Their workhouse was situated at Oversley Green. Most villages were attached to the Union of their nearest market town. In 1836 the Board of Guardians was appointed for Webheath, who were responsible for the relief of those in need and if necessary those to be sent to the new workhouse. By the 1840s the building in Pumphouse Lane had become a farmhouse and the adjoining fields were being farmed, the tenant of the property being a John Callow,[33] although by 1851 the tenancy was held by John Parker. In the upper part of a room adjoining Pumphouse Farm the Sunday School was held. This was described as the Pumphouse Schoolroom and was a large red brick room consisting of two storeys, given in 1947 by the Earl and Countess of Plymouth for the use of the church. It was also used for groups such as guides and brownies as well as Webheath Parish Council meetings. The room had a bell on top.

In the Feckenham side of the parish of Webheath there were almshouses situated on what is now Birchfield Road because the outlying parts of the parish were too far from the centre of Feckenham, so provision was made to look after the sick and elderly there. Other almshouses were situated in Astwood Bank.[34]

Although workhouses had been built to accommodate those in need, they were very unpopular and feared. Most people would try and do their best not be an inmate. Those who were sent to the workhouse were those unfortunates who could not look after themselves. The sick, the aged, orphaned or abandoned children made up the largest proportion of the inmates. Not all people were sent to the workhouse. There was flexibility in the system whereby many were given what was described as 'outdoor relief', where money or food such as bread was given, in kind, to maintain them until trade conditions improved and they could be employed. After 1840, we get references to paupers living in Webheath, applying to the Feckenham Board of Guardians for help. For example in 1841 Ann Allard, 18 years of age was given 9/- 6d. The amounts distributed varied

---

32 WRO BA11520 989:465.
33 Tithe Award Map, Tardebigge.
34 Tithe Award Map, Feckenham.

depending on the age and circumstances of the individual. It was usually an amount of money plus a loaf or loaves of bread.[35]

This ecclesiastical division of the parish into parts, one part being in Feckenham and the other part in Tardebigge, often caused problems – especially when it meant that the Board of Guardians had to pay for those people who had no means of support. There is a very telling account of one such person, named Mrs. Rowley who lived in Birchfield Road. On September 24th 1904 she came before the Bench and complained that her husband had deserted her, the complaint being that Mr. Hulland, the relieving officer had declined to assist her in getting 'out relief' for herself and her children. (Out relief meant having financial assistance at home and not being sent to the Workhouse.)

> 'Mr. Hulland told the bench the woman had made applications to him for out relief many times before but he had told her on each occasion that it was impossible for him to grant it, as The Bromsgrove Guardians had decided not to grant out relief for women deserted by their husbands.'

He advised her to go to the Workhouse and he would then try to find out her proper settlement and if she had any friends. He was of the opinion she really belonged to the Alcester Union (the Union of which Feckenham was a part) and it was only an action of justice that she should come before the Bench. She said 'She was determined not to go to the Union again and the laws of England did not necessitate a woman of good character going to the Union.' She complained they would not even allow her bread for herself and her children when she was out of work.

Mr. Hulland said 'that he was only obeying the orders of the Board'. The Chairman of the Bench said that if she did not go into the [Work] House, we cannot help you. The applicant replied by saying that if she goes into the Workhouse they would punish her little children by taking them away and she was not going to be separated from them if she could help it.

The Bench urged the woman that the best course would be for her to go to the Workhouse, but she replied that she would not go. At this the Bench had nothing more to say but tell her to stand down.[36] One wonders what the outcome of the sad story was.

---

35 Paupers Pay Accounts 1836-1843.
36 Redditch Indicator, 1904.

Poaching and Stealing

Poaching and stealing of all sorts of livestock were rife. An Act of 1770 whereby convicted persons could be imprisoned or flogged had little or no effect; so many local communities took matters into their own hands. A watchman could be appointed to keep a look-out and in the next twenty years 'Associations for the Prosecutions of Felons' were formed in the grouped parishes of Bromsgrove, Tardebigge, Stoke Prior, Upton Warren, Dodderhill, Hanbury, Hadzor and Crowle, as well as other groups of parishes. These conjoined parishes were able by means of subscription, to offer rewards for the apprehending and conviction of offenders over and above those approved by statute.[37]

The lock-up or Cage, a possession of every parish under the old parish constable system stood by what was 'The Elbows' public house. It was used for the temporary imprisonment of alleged offenders, before being brought in front of the local magistrates. 'The Elbows' public house was situated on the road to Burcot near Broad Green, the main road through Tardebigge.

The Local Horticultural Society

The Local Horticultural Society was formed in Tardebigge in the 1850s and it is probable that many people from Webheath would have participated. The Tardebigge Cottagers' and Horticultural Society's show was held in Hewell Park under the patronage of the Hon. R. H. Clive for Flowers, Fruit and Vegetables.

> 'Towards 6 o'clock the exhibitors took away their collections; the twenty two wagon loads of children wheeled off the ground amid the most vociferous shouts and hurrahs of their joyous burdens, and the general company gradually dispersed to their several homes.'[38]

However, like many other village shows it started off full of enthusiasm but finally ceased in 1869, although revived in 1880 and 1907. Local people exhibited a variety of fruit and vegetables and for prizes they were given 'cards' from the local hospital and friendly societies, the vegetables exhibited being sold for the benefit of charities. In return for their help towards the success of these shows, the exhibitors when sick, received tickets of admission to the hospitals and other benefits from the societies.[39]

---

37 Gaut p.182.
38 Ibid. p.296.
39 Rider Haggard p.406.

By 1907 Headless Cross and Webheath Hospital Societies had amalgamated. The Society at Foxlydiate was approached with a view of them joining the larger society but they decided not to and instead decided to hold a show on the grounds near Foxlydiate House with the name Foxlydiate and Hewell Flower Show Society, as reported in the *Indicator* of June 1907. In July 1907 however, The Webheath, Headless Cross, Foxlydiate and District Hospital Society held a rose show, which was held at the Rose and Crown Hotel, Webheath. The 'Rose and Crown' had graduated by now to being classed as an hotel!

Hospital and Friendly Societies

These were set up to ensure that the small tradesmen, artisans or labourers could insure themselves against sickness, unemployment or funeral expenses. Many Friendly Societies, including some very large ones, have a head office with local branch agencies. There was also the rise of the Orders, the Independent Order of Oddfellows being one of the oldest. Other fraternal organisations included the Ancient Order of Foresters. By 1873 there was a Working Man's Club, but we are not sure where it was held in Webheath, and also a Society called 'The Independent Order of Good Templars'.[40] The period 1910 to World War II saw great changes in the role of the Friendly Societies, largely because of the advent of national insurance.

Enclosure and Industry

Changing methods of agriculture meant that the old open field system, commons and wastes, where people farmed communally had to alter. Enclosure of the old commons and wastes and open fields had made improvements possible in stock breeding, land use, and rotation of crops. But, it also led to the dispossession of poorer farmers and to agrarian discontent among labourers, although it is not clear whether this happened in Tardebigge.

When Redditch and Webheath Commons were enclosed by an Act of Parliament in 1771, the old 'common' rights were destroyed and owners of them were compensated by receiving grants of land. The Earl of Plymouth received some of the common land situated in and belonging to Cutford Farm (which had been absorbed into Holyoakes Farm). The rest of the Award was divided up between about fifty individuals, many of the plots being very small in size. The largest individual award was a total of 36 acres 2 rods 22 perches to William Callow.

---

40 Needle District Almanak 1879/84.

If beasts belonging to local farmers strayed off their owner's land, they were kept in the village pound until their owner came to collect them. The one for Webheath was situated at the top of the hill on Birchfield Road, at Foxlydiate.

We know that Redditch was already involved in the making of needles and the dwellings for many of the people employed in the industry, must have encroached on the commons and waste still remaining in Redditch and Webheath. This would not have been discouraged, since every time this took place the Lord of the Manor – Lord Windsor, would have benefited, by payment of a fine to do so. In the succeeding years Lord Windsor acquired some of the former enclosed areas which he may have wanted to develop. At the same time the public roads were laid out leading to and from the hamlet of Redditch. This enclosure left much ground unenclosed, even in Redditch itself. In 1812 there was 'common' at Unicorn Hill and adjoining Evesham Street. The last remains of the old Redditch Green, is the ground around St. Stephen's Church, now laid out as a garden.[41] It is interesting to note that in 1997, the present Lord of the Manor was contacted over a dispute between Redditch Council and Hemmings the estate agents, over the piece of 'common' land between Unicorn Hill and Bates Hill. Although the Lord of the Manor does not strictly own the 'common' land it is still under his care and he is approached if there are any disputes.[42]

The Ridgeway, part of which used to be called the Bromsgrove Road and Alcester Road, has always been an important road. It has also had several different names; in its present form running from Headless Cross to Foxlydiate, it is now called Birchfield Road, but in the Census for 1851, parts of it were called Alcester Road, and Bromsgrove Road. In the seventeenth century coaches were travelling to and from London along it and there were various toll houses. It still runs parallel to the Bromsgrove Highway, across the Highway at the Foxlydiate Garage to continue on to Bromsgrove, turning left at 'The Tardebigge' pub, which was originally the village hall for Tardebigge, built by the Earl of Plymouth in 1911. The Bromsgrove Highway was opened in 1979 by Mrs. Madge Guise, a long standing resident of Webheath, a leading member of the St. John's Ambulance Brigade and the Royal British Legion.

---

41 MD p.98.
42 Redditch Advertiser, October 1997.

Mrs. Madge Guise opening Bromsgrove Highway, 1979.

The Nineteenth Century

The Victoria County History described Webheath as being just over 2,000 acres, with only 400 acres which were good enough for arable land, the rest was grass (400 acres corresponds to roughly 850 hectares). As already stated, up to the early 1800s Webheath was a mainly agrarian economy, but with the coming of industry to Redditch and the surrounding villages, the population of Webheath began to rise. From 1813, people's abode was listed in parish registers, and in Feckenham's Parish Registers, we learn that there were needlemakers living in Webheath. We can see the development of Webheath reflected in the age of the new arrivals as some of the people listed in the registers were very young, suggesting they had come in search of work.

One of the first population accounts we have[43] is a population account of Redditch and Tardebigge for 1821/31. Even in ten years we see a change in the composition of the Tardebigge side of Webheath. In 1821 there were 76 families employed in agriculture, 50 in trades and 17 in other occupations. In ten years, the number of houses had risen from 136 to 160 and the occupational structure had also changed. The number of families employed in agriculture had decreased to 52, those in trades had risen to 84 while those in other occupations changed to 26. The total number of persons had risen from 705 to 731. Webheath in 1831 – which is described as a Liberty – had 160 inhabited houses containing 162 families. There were 13 uninhabited houses, probably built with the expectation that more people would move into the parish.

---

43 WRO BA8552/4 b:850 population account 1821 Redditch and Tardebigge.

An analysis of the 1851 Census of that part of Webheath around the now enclosed common, shows that many families had moved into the neighbourhood, most of whom came from either Feckenham or Tardebigge. Only one family came from Long Crendon (another needle making centre), but as one would expect there were groups from Alcester, Studley and Sambourne. Of the rest, they were mostly men who had come from a variety of places in search of work. Most of the men and women were employed in the needle industry, whose job classifications covered every aspect of the making of needles, each one requiring a specialist skill. Many of whom would have been outworkers, carrying on their particular skills at home.

'By 1840 the quantity manufactured has increased with unexampled rapidity, the number of establishments for manufacturing needles in Redditch and Feckenham, having increased from thirty-six, in 1828 to fifty-seven in 1840; and perhaps an equal increase has been made in the quantity of needles made, which is now estimated at fifteen millions each week; or on average about 750 million annually… They are made from steel wire of the proper thickness, cut first into lengths sufficient to make two, then rough pointed and groove below the eye stamped; after which both eyes are pierced by one very quick ingenious operation, in which an error of the 10,000th part of an inch would spoil the article. From fifty to 100 of these double needles are then strung on small wires, a wire going through each eye. The burr raised on the side of the needles, by stamping and piercing, is filed off this number by one operation, and they are then separated, between the two eyes, by the file and the thick ends of each row of the needles smoothed. The eye of each needle is afterwards drilled and polished; the needle is ground, polished, hardened, blue pointed, scoured; all that are crooked, stretched and then sorted and papered ready for sale. Each of these operations requires a great deal of skill.'[44]

This information was supplied by Mr. W. Hemming, one of the important needle manufacturers, whose businesses were based on Prospect Hill and at Bordesley. The factory on Prospect Hill made needles and fish hooks, while the factory at Forge Mill Bordesley, was the needle scouring mill.

Redditch and the surrounding district had many other needle manufacturers. By the late 1880s the needle manufactories of Thomas Henry Harper and Sons and A. Townsend and Son were located at

44 Bentley's Hist. of Worcestershire Vol.VII p.108.

Webheath, in Birchfield Road,[45] both of whom would have employed many of the locals. Another important manufacturer was William Avery, whose premises were also in Birchfield Road, situated on the old Heath Springs site, now bungalows. In 1887, W. Morton Stanley is listed as a needle manufacturer,[46] while other local people were employed in the manufacture of fish hooks.

Of the agricultural workers, most were employed as farm labourers, with one substantial farmer at Green Lane Farm at Callow Hill. Mr. Palmer farmed 142 acres and employed two labourers, a house keeper, a house servant and three farm servants. As a matter of interest the descendants of Mr. Palmer still farm in the locality.

Some men worked as bricklayers; there were various brick kilns situated in the area, including one in Birchfield Road, one down Foxlydiate Lane and another situated on the old Batchley Farm; while The Ferney Heath Brickworks were situated in what is now the Bromsgrove Road (formerly Red Lane). Others were employed in glove making, as carpenters, or selling coal. The 1851 Census listed one victualler, at 'The Fox and Goose' at Foxlydiate, although we know there were other public houses by 1851. The census also listed four people who were in receipt of parish relief. Another occupation was that of 'omnibus proprietor'; an omnibus carriage was used for carrying freight as well as passengers.

As one would expect the urban area was situated along the main road now known as Birchfield Road (then a toll road to Bromsgrove) with fields and farms in the hinterland. Some of these farms have been swallowed up for housing over the last 150 years, built as the population grew, as a result of the demand for labour in the main industries; with most of the bricks for the new housing being made locally from the local clay pits.

Towards the end of the nineteenth century there was a great agricultural depression. As a result of this, various Acts were passed, including one in 1883 to help alleviate the distress caused. In 1885 an agitation began throughout the country for the provision of allotments which resulted in the founding of the Allotments and Smallholdings Association. In 1894 The Local Government Act established parish councils and part of the Act made provision of allotments for small landowners, who could then subsidise their earnings. The Smallholdings and Allotments Act of 1907 authorized County Councils to acquire land, by compulsory purchase if necessary, for the purpose of providing small holdings for bona fide applicants. This scheme enabled and encouraged people to go into

---

45 PO Directory Worcestershire, 1892.
46 Needle Trade Almanack, 1894.

farming who would otherwise not be able to do so. For many years there were allotments situated in the area behind Heathfield Road.

Worcestershire County Council purchased much land and became substantial landowners. Under this scheme they purchased The White House Farm in Love Lyne, Callow Hill, in 1912 from the Sillins estate. Barn Close Farm and Bredon View Farm, built c.1957/8, were built on land which had been part of the White House Farm. White House Farm originally consisted of about 106 acres, and it is clear from the following account which is abstracted from a book on rural England that various smallholdings were created in the Webheath district.

A short resume of the life of **H. Rider Haggard** will help to put the following account into its historical context.

H. Rider Haggard was born and educated in Norfolk. He was sent at an early age to South Africa, when, after many adventures he returned to England, married Louisa Margitson and started writing adventure stories. *King Solomon's Mines* which he wrote in 1885 was his first success and transformed his life by making him financially secure. He wanted to do something more practical, so addressed himself to the desperate state of farming in England. He kept a diary for a year (1898) which was published as *A Farmer's Year* and as a result became an agricultural authority and an expert on rural affairs.

In 1901/2 he travelled throughout England and wrote articles for the *Daily Express* on agricultural conditions. The result was *Rural England* (two volumes) published in 1902.

In 1912 he was knighted and made KBE in 1919. Haggard died in May 1925 and his remains are buried in Ditchingham Church. Haggard was described as tall and swarthy, 'a Norseman in looks' by one of his friends. He moved easily among the public figures of the time, having an acute mind, interested in the many facets of religions, re-incarnation etc.[47]

While travelling through Warwickshire, he visited Mr. S. C. Thornton Jagger, who since 1893 had been agent to the Bentley Estate, which, as he comments, lay partly in Worcestershire and partly in Warwickshire. Mr. Thornton Jagger lived at Upper Norgrove and ran the Bentley Estate from this address. Upper Norgrove is situated at the Hill Top at the end of Heathfield Road. Rider Haggard mentions Webheath and the various smallholders in the parish, including Mr. James, a fish hook maker with a large family, who had an allotment of a quarter of an acre, which he rented for 18s. a year. On it he grew a variety of vegetables which helped feed his family. The rent of a cottage was between £4-£5 a year and might include

47 Oxford DNB Vol.24 pp.443-5 Ed. H.C.G. Matthew OUP 2004.

a garden or allotment worth 10s. a year. Another small farmer named Mr. *Bartland* (Bartlam) hired thirty acres at a rent of £48 a year growing various crops and keeping cows, the milk from which he made butter, selling it at 1s.3d a pound. He made a profit from his pigs and, as he had a nice house, took the local curate in as a lodger. Mr. Haggard goes on to mention Mr. Thomas Neasom who was the land agent and auctioneer in Redditch. Neasom and White were the local estate agents and auctioneers in Redditch for over 137 years until 1993 when Mr. David Thomas, Thomas Neasom's grandson, retired. David Thomas remembers his uncle commenting on meeting Rider Haggard, who by this time had a long white beard and moustache.

Ecclesiastical Districts, Parish Church, Parish Council

With the rise in population new ecclesiastical districts were formed. In 1850, part of Webheath, some of Ipsley and Feckenham were amalgamated to become the district of St. Lukes at Headless Cross. At this time most of Webheath was part of the parish of Tardebigge, but it was decided that Webheath needed a church of its own. To further this need, the major landowners of the parish, who were the Windsor family at Hewell Grange and the Hemmings at Bentley Manor, donated land and money to build what is now St. Philip's Church. In 1869 Baroness Windsor gave a dinner at the 'Fox and Goose' for the fifty workpeople engaged in building the new church. The church was built at a cost of just over £3,000, given by the Baroness, on land given by Mr. R. H. Hemming JP of Bentley Manor. The church was designed by Mr. F. Preedy in the early English style with seating all unappointed for 200 (many pews in churches at this time were set aside, or 'appointed' for various prominent local families who paid for the privilege). The building was constructed with red and grey stone from the local quarries at Hewell and Finstall with Bath stone dressings and decorations. Various memorials in **St. Philips** church have been donated by members of the congregation, including the *Royal British Legion Rolls of Honour*, which lists the names of the fallen of two World Wars.

The *Rolls of Honour* to the fallen in the two World Wars are situated on the west wall of church:

1914-1918

T.E. Alexander	W. Futrill
J.W. Andrews	E. Gibbs
O. Andrews	F. Griffin
A. Barker	B. Harper
T. Beckensale	A. Harris
H.M. Bowen	E.T. Hawthorne
G. Broom	E.F. Hunt
H.G. Cheape	S. James
L.S. Cheape	J.C. Lee
A.J. Clayton	E. Morris
A.W. Clayton	J. Smout
C. Futrill	T. Such

F. Waters

1939-1945

Stanley Barter	Eric Melley
Fred Fletcher	Edward Rickards

Kenneth Smith

Palestine 1948

William Robinson

The Register of Baptisms commences in 1870 and the Register of Marriages from 1939. The Parsonage is situated opposite the church, on land donated by Lord Plymouth in 1920/21. This plot is now up for sale to be re-developed into six dwellings including a new parsonage on part of the plot. It is being sold by Humberts, as the agents (2007). At the side of the Parsonage was a tennis court on land given by Mr. Howard Bird in 1946. The ecclesiastical parish of St. Philip's was formed in 1982, with its own vicar. Until this time it had been a mission church of St. Bartholomew's Tardebigge.

There was also a Baptist Chapel at Webheath in Birchfield Road. **The Baptists** are a non-conformist sect who believes in spiritual regeneration through adult baptism. Their place of worship is now used as a church for the Christadelphians. By 1873 there was a Working Mens Club, situated in Webheath Lane and a Society, one of many in the Redditch area, called The Independent Order of Good Templars.

Queen Victoria's Jubilee in 1873 was celebrated in Webheath as in most towns and villages. It was held on a Tuesday and a committee

Photograph courtesy WRO Photographic Survey.

Baptist Chapel, Birchfield Road, c.1966.

was chosen for the purpose, who issued tickets to about 200 adults and children. At three o'clock the children partook of a substantial tea under a tent in a field adjoining the 'Rose and Crown'. The meal included beef, ham, cake etc., and each child was also presented with a medal and a gift of some kind. At 4.30p.m. the adults sat down to a similar fare at the 'Rose and Crown' Assembly Room, and the more aged persons were presented with a packet of tea or an ounce of tobacco and a 3 pence check (or token) for any refreshments they preferred. Several races were provided for elderly people, youths and children. At 9.30p.m. the very little ones were taken in wagons to view the bonfire in the 'Soudan' (a field, which is now part of the municipal golf course) and returned about 10.30p.m. singing The National Anthem, all seeming to have thoroughly enjoyed themselves.[48]

Webheath Parish Council was formed as a result of the Local Government Act of 1894. It met regularly, usually at the Pumphouse Lane Schoolroom, but also at Tardebigge Village Hall until 1930, when, under the provisions of the Worcestershire (Redditch Urban District) Confirmation Order, the greater portion of the parish was transferred to the parish and urban district of Redditch.[49]

---

48 Redditch Indicator, 1887.
49 Kelly's Directory, 1940.

The 'Rose and Crown', Webheath.

The Twentieth Century

At the early part of the twentieth century Webheath is described as:

> 'A village, situate partly in the township of Webheath and partly in the parish of Feckenham. The village is distant one mile south-west of Redditch Railway Station, two miles south-east of Tardebigge Church, and 16 miles south of Birmingham. The township of Webheath which takes its name from the village, forms a part of the ancient parish of Tardebigge and is partly in that ecclesiastical district and partly in the ecclesiastical district of St. Lukes, Headless Cross; it is in the rural district and Union of Bromsgrove, the Stoke Prior Electoral Division of Worcestershire, the mid or Droitwich Parliamentary Division, Upper Halfshire Hundred, and Redditch County Court District. The Earl of Plymouth is Lord of the Manor – which says it all!'[50]

As Webheath and Redditch grew, more facilities appeared. The new post office was opened in what is now Heathfield Road on the corner of the fore-draught, run by Eliza While c.1902. Walter French had opened a greengrocer's shop in Birchfield Road, with Mr. James running a butcher's

---

50 Needle Trade Almanack, 1919.

shop in Webheath Lane and Benjamin Lee was listed as a shopkeeper at Foxlydiate, subsequently the sub-post office. Sporting activities were represented with a local cricket club formed in 1905. The political scene also dominated the local news, with reports of many politicians visiting the locality. In 1908 an address was given by Mr. Lyttelton, a former Colonial Secretary under Balfour, while the subject of the emancipation of women achieved a lot of local interest. Lady Isabel Margesson held meetings in connection with women's emancipation at Foxlydiate House, where the Margessons lived at the time. (Sir Montague Margesson 1861-1947, was private secretary to the Earl of Plymouth.) They must have moved soon after, as Mr. McCandlish is listed as residing at Foxlydiate House in 1910, but the Margessons were still living locally in 1928. Webheath was certainly important enough to have its own police officer who was based at 'Lewisvale' in Church Road. In 1910, the local 'bobbie' was James Broom.

On May 15th 1902 a murder was committed in what was then called Springhill Lane (Foxlydiate Lane). At about 2 o'clock in the morning Mrs. Hannah Middleton was murdered by her husband, a hay trusser who came home very drunk, killed his wife and set fire to the cottage together with the adjoining one. It is said that he covered her with straw, took a flitch of bacon off the wall, covered her in bacon fat and set fire to her. Middleton was arrested during the day in Trenches Lane, Himbleton. He subsequently confessed to the crime, was tried at Worcester Assizes and executed at Worcester Gaol on July 15th 1902.

In a letter to the *Redditch Advertiser* October 18th 1995, a lady, whose grandmother lived next door to the murdered lady in Foxlydiate Lane; quoted a rhyme recounting the tale which went,

> 'Her name was Middleton.
> The policeman who caught him was Billington.
> He was caught at Himbleton.'

As Webheath expanded more houses were built in Heathfield Road and along the Birchfield Road; the village was becoming more important – a post box was sited on the corner of Heathfield Road and there was a smithy next door to the Baptist chapel,[51] a most important facility at the time when the horse was a most important means of travel. Some people always bemoan change, whatever the circumstances or whichever century, and this expansion resulted in an article in the *Redditch Indicator* c.1911, sent in by an anonymous resident – describing himself as 'Rustic'.

51 Ordnance Survey Map, 1888.

'I was born in the village – as a matter of fact in the lane. To be quite precise, I should say in a house in the lane.

Ever since my perceptive powers began to develop I have been an ardent student of human nature, and for nearly a quarter of a century I studied that human nature which moved and had its being in our village. My conclusions were that the chief characteristic of our village was modesty.

Our parish council was composed of modest men. If they were debating the momentous question of whether a stile needed repairing or whether the clap gate should be painted black or white, they were careful that only a modest sum should be voted for the purpose.

There was a modest village inn, where "the rude forefathers of the hamlet" were wont to gather when the day was done, and over pipe and beer talk on modest things. The village church was modest too. When it rose up it modestly withdrew itself into the shadow of the giant beeches that, sentinel like, watch over it.

The houses in the lane are modest. When the winds of wintry nights shriek and howl around them like the wailing of lost souls doomed to eternal torment; when the rain lashes itself in a mad fury against them, the windows in their modesty, open of their own accord, and gracefully bow to the majesty of the elements.

One cottage at the end of the lane was perhaps the most modest of all. It was the same cottage where I always called to show off my modest new suits – never forgetting to examine the pockets in the trousers to see if a modest coin had been dropped in. On the portals of this cottage rude hands had carved the date 1656AD. From the time that Cromwell was tottering to his fall until the Insurance Act came into force this cottage had stood and watched the progress of our modest village.

There was never any gossiping in our village. Nobody worried themselves about other people's affairs.

You will notice that for the most part I have written in the past tense. Am I admitting then, that our modesty is something that has gone into the limbo of forgotten things? Alas, alas, it is so. How did it happen? It was like this.

The lane was cut up and a sewage scheme was laid. Then some blue bricks were put down in parts to keep the pathways from slipping into the road – I should say lane. Then a Post Office appeared in the lane. Once again there was a disturbance of earth and gas mains were laid down, the result being that the modest oil lamp retired from the place of honour it had held for so many years. Now the erstwhile calm and peaceful solitude of the lane is disturbed by the snorting and puffing of mighty gas engines that make the air hideous with their noises.

My old modest cottage fell into the rapacious and capacious maw of the jerry-builder. Not a brick not a beam now remains. On its ruins have been raised some cheap and ugly looking things called houses; and in the summer where once the birds made glad the long summer days with their songs of joy, is only heard the hideous wailing of twenty five shilling gramophones. The modest daffodils and snowdrops that peeped so modestly from under the hedgerows in springtime have been ruthlessly uprooted or buried beneath bricks and mortar.

The inn is now an hotel where men gather and discuss philosophy with such consummate ease that old Socrates must grow envious in his age worn sepulchre. The laws of gravitation are explained and demonstrated with a lucidity that does our master minds the highest credit.

Is it to be wondered at, then, that with a Parish Council, a sewage scheme, a post office, an hotel, gas, and gas engines and a male voice choir, the lane itself became dissatisfied with the insignificant appellation "Lane"? One gentleman saw justification for its grievance; took it before the controlling body, and, to all posterity, through the ages that are to come, before the sun shall give no more warmth and light to our planet, **Webheath Lane** is to be known as **Heathfield Road**.

Alas for our lost prestige. We are snobs now. **Heathfield Road!** Were it not so snobbish how funny it would be; how deliciously humorous? "Lane" may serve the purpose in a small sleepy place like London; but in a progressive village it will not do!'

Some of Heathfield Road so described, was part of the 'Sillins' estate, which was sold in 1912. 'Sillins' was the home of the Haywood family, and the main house still exists, situated at Callow Hill. The sale attracted much interest, with many lots sold, while other lots were sold privately. The sale realised £25,000. Some of the properties which were situated in Webheath included; a group of four houses known as Major's Row in Heathfield Road; Sycamore Farm, then known as Hill Top Farm; the cottage on the corner of Crumpfields Lane; [what were] the fields along the east side of Heathfield Road and Crumpfields Farm. These fields now have houses and bungalows on them.

Britain entered what is often called the Great War on 4th August 1914. It affected everyone's lives. Local men were called upon to volunteer for the armed forces, as they were everywhere else. Those who lost their lives from Webheath are immortalised in a plaque outside St. Philip's Church and a list of men who lost their lives was printed each week in the *Redditch Indicator*. There were threats of raids by Zeppelins but, luckily, they passed near to the town without doing any damage. There was much emphasis on food economy and Food Control Committees were appointed throughout the district; to these was given authority to fix the prices of various foods and other necessaries. Towards the end of the war it was clear that there was a shortage of certain articles and many queues of people could be seen waiting their chance to obtain goods. To encourage people to grow their own food, land was broken up into allotments. Lighting and Fuel Economy committees were also set up; many of the streets were unlit and the shops closed an hour early.

Locally, people still celebrated Empire Day on 24th May, and in August 1917 a War Shrine was unveiled at Webheath Church by Archbishop Peile. One of the members of the Gray-Cheape family, Col. Cheape (of Bentley Manor) was reported missing in May 1918 when returning home on 'The Leasowes Castle' which was torpedoed. After the war ended a meeting was held to consider the proposal to build a house for the curate of Webheath, as well as a proposal to have a war memorial to commemorate the fallen. As a result of this the parsonage was built c.1920/21.

July 19th was Peace Celebration Day and great celebrations took place around St. Stephen's Church, Redditch as well as in other town and village centres.

1939-1945

On September 3rd 1939 war on Germany was declared. Local provisions for possible invasion were put into place, as it had been apparent for sometime that local defences would have to be organized, especially around key sites such as factories making armaments, like BSA Ipsley; High Duty Alloys, Windsor Road, or work for the Ministry of Supply at the Enfield Cycle Company, Redditch. (For a complete list of companies see *The Defence of Worcestershire* by Mick Wilks.) Royal Enfield, where many local people worked, had developed various brilliant devices, among them were the oil units for the Bofor anti-air craft guns, which were operated by the sound of a plane. Whichever way the sound came from the gun faced that way and fired at the noise.[52]

People may not have realized that Worcestershire was the scene of so much military activity, and complex preparations for defence were put into

---

52 Anne Bradford, Royal Enfield. p.43.

place.[53] As part of the preparations for an invasion, direction signs were removed from roads and railways to make life difficult for any invading forces. (See copy of maps for the Home Guard.)

There were three primary elements of defence, which were; a defence of the potential landing beaches around Britain; a line of defence which was designed to protect London and the industrial Midlands and the North and a strategic reserve of the Field Army. In addition to these three primary elements, there were defended nodal points or anti-tank islands, all intended to obstruct or delay enemy armoured columns. Since the enemy would have had to use the main roads to advance, and most roads in those days ran through the middle of towns, main towns and cities were designated as 'anti-tank islands'[54] which included Redditch. In those 'islands' all potential landing grounds were to be obstructed. With manpower numbers of around 19,000 men the largest single static force in the county was the LDV/Home Guard who would garrison the majority of fixed defences.[55]

In Redditch it was the "C" Company, 9th Worcestershire (Redditch Battalion Home Guard). "C" Company's territory covered the villages of Crabbs Cross, Headless Cross, Hewell and Webheath. Individual platoons within the Company were responsible for specific villages or areas. The company consisted of four platoons comprising 20-30 men in each platoon and their Company headquarters were located over the former Alcester Co-op at Headless Cross, a building now occupied by Morris's

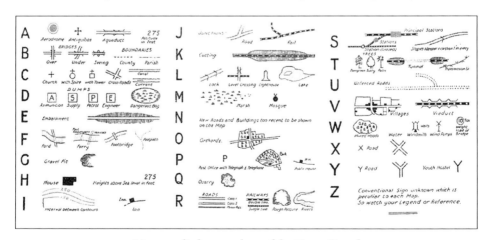

Map supplied to members of the Home Guard.

53 Wilkes Defence of Worcestershire. p.xii.
54 Ibid. p.15.
55 Ibid. p.39.

shop. They played a very important part in the defence of the area. They manned the telephone at HQ and the local roadblocks, as well as receiving training on the use of firearms and hand grenades. Nearly every weekend was taken up by training exercises, carried out in various locations including Musketts Wood. "C" Company, as with other companies in the battalion, had to provide men for night duty at the Reynolds Tubes – now Alcan.[56]

Other static units were The Royal Warwickshire Regiment and Military Police who would contribute to the manning of defences. Ron Batson recollects that his father was in the Home Guard. During the day his father worked at BSA making guns and in the evening was on fire watch duty.

Communal air-raid shelters were a common sight during war time. These were built in various sizes to accommodate 25, 50 or 100 persons, one of which stood at Hill Top on the corner of Church Road and Heathfield Road. The former site is now occupied by houses. There were numerous other shelters situated around Redditch and Webheath, including a number of shelters in Birchfield Road, and three in Heathfield Road, which included one at the Village Hall and another at Hill Top.[57] Other air-raid shelters for family use were the Morrison and Anderson shelters. The Anderson shelter, synonymous with the Blitz, was erected in

Photograph courtesy WRO Photographic Survey.

Musketts Way, 1966.

---

56 Mike Johnson. The story of "C" Co. 9th Worc. (Redditch) Battalion Home Guard.
57 Information kindly provided by Mike Johnson.

people's gardens. The Morrison shelter was erected inside people's homes. It was designed for use by people without gardens and was approximately 6ft 6ins long, 4ft wide and 2ft 6ins high. The shelter, made from heavy steel could also be used as a table. (The author remembers her parents' shelter being used for a variety of uses – including a make-shift stage. At night, one went to bed underneath the shelter.) The theory behind the Morrison shelter was that should the house collapse while using the Morrison shelter, then those inside would be able to crawl out from under the debris.

One of the fields or hams that had obstructions to deter landings, was on the old Golf Course at Redditch, then situated in Plymouth Road. Rough hewn wooden poles were erected so that 12 feet of each pole stuck out of the ground and the effect was a small forest of poles. Concrete blocks were also used at Redditch. Two other large fields elsewhere were obstructed with poles; one to the south of Salters Lane, another to the east of the BSA factory. There were probably others.[58] There were trenches and a road block at the edge of Foxlydiate Wood in Birchfield Road, all part of the system of defences, designed to protect Redditch's key points from attack.[59]

The war finally ended in 1945 and many streets up and down the land held street parties to celebrate. At Upper Norgrove, Hill Top, the home of Mr. and Mrs. Ludford, a party was held for the local children in Webheath.

In August 1948, *The Redditch Advertiser* reported on provisional plans for the development of Webheath as a residential centre, which were outlined by George White, Webheath representative on Redditch Urban District Council, at a meeting of Webheath British Legion Branch. Maps, displayed at the meeting by E. Buckley, surveyor, contained proposals for the creation of three new roads, the provision of a cinema site, licensed premises, sports field and community club.

The outline proposals for the future development of the area were described as unofficial… The local authority had purchased land which was previously owned by the Plymouth Estates and it was the council's intention to negotiate for the acquisition of two remaining fields…

In view of a report received from the council's town planning consultant, Sir Patrick Abercrombie, this scheme had been somewhat modified. Well, as we know, the houses were built but it is not clear what happened about the rest of the proposals!

---

58 Wilkes p.62.
59 Ibid. pp.116/17.

Reminiscences of old Webheath

The author is very grateful to Ruby Gardner and David Thomas, both long time residents of Webheath, who have contributed to so much of the following information. Some reminiscences are of the 20s and 30s, while other information germane to the district has been incorporated.

Ruby was born and bred in Webheath. When she was three, her family moved to Valley Cottage, which her father had built in 1925. Ruby's father was a gamekeeper at Bentley Manor and had originally worked at Eastnor Castle.

Because there was no local school the children used to have to walk two or three miles, either to Bentley which was an Infants' School, to Tardebigge which took children up to the age of fourteen, or Headless Cross. Later on, the children went to Holyoakes School – then called the 'tin school' in Bridge Street. If children lived in Church Road they would go to Tardebigge as they were in the parish of Tardebigge catchment area.

Most people worked locally, either in Redditch, Headless Cross or Crabbs Cross. Some people went into service. Ruby worked first at Rudges, the fishing rod and tackle makers, British Needles, and then Terry's until she was married, then at Sealey's, rod finishing until she had her two boys. Ruby has lived in a variety of houses in Webheath, she moved into what is now 66 Heathfield Road in 1949 and lived there until recently, when she moved to Terry Springs Court.

At first the footpaths in Heathfield Road were just made of ashes, put down originally by the residents, but later on, the ashes were supplied by the Council. In fact Heathfield Road was not made up until just before the Second World War, one reason being that one half of the road the Sycamore Farm side, was in the parish of Feckenham and the other side in Tardebigge, so there was a division of responsibility.

When Ruby and John first moved in to no.66 there was no running water, just a stand pipe for all the cottages, until the houses were connected to the mains. The night soil man used to come round once a week to empty the privies, which were situated in the garden next door to the wash house. At this time the gardens were not fenced off individually but were communal. Each house had a wash house, where the weekly wash was done. The water was heated underneath by a boiler. These cottages were owned by Ruby's uncle Percy Carr and at the back of the cottages was a turkey farm, while at the back of the other end of what is now Heathfield Road were allotments. These allotments used to have box hedging, which was cut regularly and sold. The men were always given lunch at the double fronted cottage opposite where Grandma Carr (Ruby's grandmother) used to live at Hill Top.

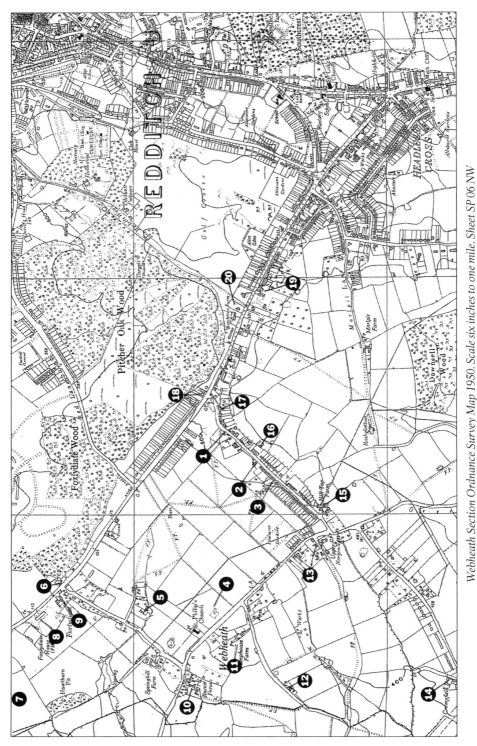

Webheath Section Ordnance Survey Map 1950. Scale six inches to one mile. Sheet SP 06 NW

KEY 1. Village Hall. 2. Poultry Farm. 3. Old Post Office. 4. 'Saltways' Leonard Cheshire Home. 5. Springvale Cottages. 6. Site of 'Fox & Goose' and old P.O. 7. Tack Cottages. 8. Site of Foxlydiate House. 9. Foxlydiate Farm. 10. Boxnott Farm 11. Pumphouse Farm. 12. Saw Mill. 13. Three Cottages. 14. Crumpfields Farm. 15. Hill Top/Sycamore Farm. 16. The 'Tin House'. 17. The 'Rose and Crown'. 18. 'Biddles' Convenience Store. 19. Site of 'T. Harper and Sons'. 20. Birch Tree Farm/Musketts Way. This is not a definitive map.

Most of the development in Webheath has occurred since the Second World War. Originally, Webheath consisted of a few scattered cottages many of which have now disappeared. As we go down Heathfield Road from Birchfield Road, there was a cottage before the Village Hall (1), lived in by Mrs. Ball. The land for the Village Hall was bought by Mr. Victor Woodfield. He gave it to the village, with £180 from church funds used to go towards the cost of the wooden building, which was built around 1925. Originally it had a bowling green at the back, which is now converted into a car park.

Downsell Road did not exist, that area was just farm land, with a farm called 'The Heath', owned by Mr. Bawcutt, then Mr. Weaver, who ran it as a poultry farm (2). The area now covered with houses used to belong to the Earl of Plymouth and after he died in 1943 the whole estate was put up for sale, including what was originally the common. It was scheduled to be bought by three men but, at the last minute Redditch District Council stepped in and bought it.

As we continue down Heathfield Road towards the Post Office some of the original cottages have disappeared and modern houses and bungalows have been built in their place. Then we come to the row of cottages next door to the present post office – one of which is where Ruby and John lived. The original post office (3) was further along on the corner of the fore draught and was run by the Misses While. Some of the houses further down the road were built in the 1930s by a builder called C. J. Huins. As we turn the corner into Hill Top, there were some more scattered cottages and two at the bottom of the valley, which was very wet and boggy, so much so that bullrushes grew there. There was a cottage near where 'Saltways' now is. 'Saltways' (4), a Leonard Cheshire Home, was built in 1975. Next we come to the church of St. Philips, in which is a Reredos, donated by the Rt. Hon. Robert Clive and a Communion Set by Canon C. A. Dickens, a former Vicar of Tardebigge. In Foxlydiate Lane on the right-hand side there were and are three cottages called Springvale Cottages (5), which lie behind the thatched cottage. These three cottages now have five modern houses built (c.2000) in the front gardens of the old plots. A lady called Rhona Harris lived in the cottages for many years and often helped out at the little shack when it was a shop (known as The Woodland Stores), as well as the egg farm at Tardebigge. After the modern development of houses (see notes on Foxlydiate Farm) we come up to Foxlydiate, where there are three cottages called Boxnott Cottages, while opposite was the Fox and Goose Pub, run in the 20s and 30s by the Chambers family. Next door was Foxlydiate Post Office (6) and shop which had a tea room attached. Mr. Benjamin Lee is listed in 1901 as running the shop.

Photograph courtesy WRO Photographic Survey.

The Woodland Stores, Foxlydiate Lane, Foxlydiate, c.1966.

Mr. and Mrs. Benjamin Lee had three sons Fred, Ernest and Jess, and two daughters. After Mr. Lee died Mrs. Lee ran the Post Office until 1929 when she was succeeded by her daughter Mrs. Humphries. Mrs. Humphries lived until 1980, to the marvellous age of 86 years. Harold Humphries her husband, who was employed by the Bromsgrove Guild, died in July 1949 after a long illness. He was a member of a team responsible for the making and hanging of the wrought iron gates at Buckingham Palace. It is interesting to note that the beautifully designed lock on the Palace gates bears the names of Mr. McCandlish and Mr. Pancheri. It was Mr. McCandlish, who married Miss Fry of the chocolate family and who lived at Foxlydiate House, who arranged employment for Harold at the Bromsgrove Guild. Fred Lee, one of the brothers, (Madge Guise's father) worked for the British Needle Company.[60]

Crossing over the other side of the road, we proceed up the hill to Hill and Tack Farms (7) which in the 1930s were owned by Dr. Houfton. Hill Farm is first mentioned in the seventeenth century as being occupied by a Mr. D'Abitot.[61] By this time the Hill Farm was known as Tack Cottages. Mr. and Mrs. David and Molly Thomas now live in the modern house called Hunter's Hill, built on the site of Tack Cottages. A Mr. Hughes lived there at one time.

'The Foxlydiate' pub was built on the site of the old Foxlydiate House (8) which in the 1930s was owned by Mr. and Mrs. McCandlish (see

---

60 I am indebted to Madge Guise for the information, re the Lee family.
61 Prattinton Collection pp.16-17.

Foxlydiate House, c.1935.

note about Foxlydiate House) and was pulled down in the 1930s. During the First World War, Foxlydiate House was used as a soup kitchen. Foxlydiate House was built by W. Hemming the son of the founder of the needlemaking dynasty. He died in 1849 when it then formed part of the Bentley estate. When the pub was built, it was officially opened by Evelyn Laye – the famous musical star. A later house, situated up the hill, also known as Foxlydiate House, now pulled down, was owned by the Sealey family. Then we come to Foxlydiate Farm (9) which was farmed by Mr. Shrimpton and was sold off in the last twenty years. The Woodland Stores (now a boarded up little shack) next door was used as a shop as well as a butchers for some time. Following along the road we come to three cottages, and in the end one a murder took place, as previously described. A man killed his wife and put her in the kitchen with a flitch of bacon on top to hide the deed and set fire to the cottage but he was found out. There is a modern wood yard next door run by Billy Hatful.

Then we have Springhill Farm which used to be owned by Mr. Howard Hill. His son was a butcher and in the summer their grounds were used to hold pageants in which the local children took part. Opposite the end of Foxlydiate Lane was Boxnott Farm (10), last farmed by Arthur Partridge,

Photograph courtesy Alan Foxall.

'Squire' Haywood.

Webheath Post Office Stores, 2000.

then before by Mr. and Mrs. Walker and recently sold. The farmhouse was pulled down c.1997 and 210 houses have been erected on the farm land. There used to be an old cottage next door to the Parsonage. The Parsonage was built in 1921 with money raised by the parishioners on land given by Lord Plymouth. There was a portion of land adjoining the Parsonage used as a Tennis Court which was given by Mr. Howard Bird in 1946. Further along we come to Pumphouse Lane which now has eighteen houses built in the field next to Pumphouse Cottage. Next door is Pumphouse Farm (11) already mentioned, which was originally built as a workhouse. When Ruby was a girl she used to attend the Sunday School there as well as the girl guides. The local guide mistress was called Mrs. Rice who lived in Crumpfields Lane.

The Saw Mill down Pumphouse Lane, called Holborne Saw Mill, was a farm until it was converted into a saw mill by a family called Pollard who moved the saw mill from 'The Woodyard' in Church Road. Mrs. Pollard also sold coal from the Church Road site as well as wood. The big saw was then moved to Holborne Farm. The Saw Mill (12) is now run by David Partridge, formerly of Boxnott Farm. Then we pass Holly Cottage (a Holly Cottage was listed as a laundry in 1911, but there is another Holly Cottage in Heathfield Road). Continue down the valley to two or three houses, one of which, Valley Cottage, was built by Ruby's

Holborne Saw Mill.

Remains of thatched cottage, Church Road, Webheath.

father. Next door to 'The Woodyard' used to be the policeman's cottage, called 'Lewisvale'. Passing the 'Woodyard' on your right, now a garage, is the remains of what used to be a thatched cottage. Then we come to a double fronted house with a cottage attached, down the lane to Brownlass Farm. This lane was originally called Green Lane and led to Crumpfields Farm. It used to join Pumphouse Lane, but is now only a bridle path at the latter half. Next door to the original Brownlass Farm (presumably named after Henry *Brownless* who lived there in 1891) are three half-timbered cottages (13). Originally one up, one down, they are probably the oldest houses in Webheath. Nos. 3, 5, and 7 were originally three cottages, now two. Nos. 5 and 7 were made into one cottage. These three cottages were owned by Mrs. May Harris who had two sons Albert and Ivor, Albert lived in No. 3. Mrs. Radbourne the current occupier of No. 5, is Ivor Harris's daughter.

Miss W. E. Compton lived at Upper Norgrove and Kate Freeman, who was 95 years old when she died, worked there as a housemaid in the 1930s. There was also a cook and gardener called Mr. Bray who lived in the house opposite. Kate remembers going out to collect the milk from the milkman with a gill measure. Miss Compton was the first person in Webheath to own a car. Upper Norgrove then became a home for young offenders before being converted into single people's flats.

The Crest Garage, Crumpfields Lane, Webheath, c.1997.

Crumpfields Lane, is an old lane which was already in existence three hundred years ago, as shown on Doherty's map of 1591, copied in 1744.

A social survey carried out by Jim Brown, formerly of No. 2, Crumpfields Lane, in 2000 as part of a Millennium Project, was mounted and organised by Feckenham Forest History Society. He summarised his findings as follows: There are eighty-four houses in Crumpfields Lane, the oldest being a cottage now numbered No. 3 and a farmhouse called Crumpfields Farm (14). There was a service garage called The Crest Garage, owned by Mr. Claude Hims, with a forecourt with petrol pumps (now demolished with four houses built on the site), next to Crumpfields Farm. Pool Farm is situated opposite Crumpfields Farm; the buildings of which used to form part of Crumpfields Farm.

Twenty-six residents completed the questionnaire, which gave the age of the houses, the present occupiers and in some cases the previous owners. Most of the present occupiers are retired professionals: doctors, dentists, solicitors, consultants, teachers, businessmen, manufacturers, whose places of work were located in the Redditch area, as was the case with the newer but younger occupiers of the houses. The age of the houses and bungalows range from those built in 1919 to more recent developments built at the beginning of 2000.

There was, other than farming, evidence of commercial activity at one property, No. 68, which was used as a Dairy run by the Biddle family until 1959, when the premise reverted to being a residential property. Mr. Biddle took over Norman English's (Lower Grinsty Farm) milk round, as well as that run from Pools Farm, and eventually had five milk rounds.

The houses and bungalows are red brick but some have white pebble dash exteriors, their roofs being tile in the majority of cases, but some have slate. The gardens are bigger than those of many normal modern houses, reflecting the size of the properties which are mainly four and five bedroom, having double garages either part of the main building or standing separately. Most respondents had mechanical means to assist them in the garden; petrol lawnmowers, some mains electric, some battery driven. There were mains electric hedge cutters and lawn strimmers, showing how labour saving devices are extensively used, as against manual part-time labour of fifty years ago.

Kate Freeman was also interviewed for her reminiscences. After working for Miss W. E. Compton, she worked for Mrs. Rendle for many years. Mrs. Rendle (who ran The White Heather Club for many years) lived at what is now No. 31 Crumpfields Lane. Kate remembered the milk being delivered by Norman English, the farmer from Lower Grinsty Farm, when he had a local delivery round. Bread was delivered, as were blocks of salt by dray horses and vegetables by horse and cart. A man would come round to sharpen your knives and scissors. Fish and meat was also delivered.

We then turn back into Heathfield Road, where there were quite a few shops, including a general stores on the corner next door to Sycamore Farm (15), kept at one time by Mrs. Yapp. Mr. Headley Cooke of Sycamore Farm used to supply milk. The next few rows of houses were built in the middle of the nineteenth century. Facing the modern post office was a lime pit. In one of the three bungalows, Mrs. Robinson used to sell coal and hardware, while there was a shop and bakers kept by a Mrs. Shepherd opposite the old Post Office. Near to Mrs. Chambers (who lives at 109) was a grocery shop which sold grocery and fresh vegetables, run by a Mr. Partridge. Further along the road, a few doors down from Mr. and Mrs. McGovern (No. 53 then No. 43), towards The Rose and Crown, there was a butchers shop run by Mr. James and a fish and chip shop run by Mr. Spiers.

There were two cottages knocked down to make way for Middle Piece Drive. Ruby remembers that the people in these old cottages had to walk down the road to a stand pipe for their water. There was also a shop run by some people called Batty which sold pinafores, stockings and groceries. At the back of these houses was what was known as the 'Tin House' (16), occupied by the Hands family.

The Old Rose and Crown (17) had a frontage onto the road with a large club or assembly room on the first floor, used by The Webheath Royal British Legion. The pub also had a bowling green behind the premises. A Bowling Club existed in the 1930s, the Secretary and Treasurer was Mr. W. Unitt, of 66 Heathfield Road.[62] A friendly society called the Independent Order of Buffaloes used to meet there. When the new Rose and Crown was built c.1968, the bowling green was moved to the back of the Village Hall – which explains its large car park. At Harvest Time there was always a Harvest Supper provided by Mr. Hill of Springhill Farm and Mr. McCandlish of Foxlydiate House. The Village Hall was not allowed to serve alcoholic drinks until the 1960s because of a clause in the original deeds imposed by Mr. Woodfield (who donated the land) which forbade it, probably because there was a pub opposite. When there was an interval everyone used to repair to the pub. The licence was not granted until 1960s.

Where 'Biddles' (18), the convenience store in Birchfield Road opposite Heathfield Road, is now, was a bakers called Langston's. It had its own bakery, with a petrol pump on the forecourt and a hairdresser's salon above; while the lady opposite in the cottage used to sell Woodbines! Further along Birchfield Road, was a brick kiln and the Phoenix Needle Factory, the premises of T. Harper and Sons (19). Next to the chapel was a general stores run by a Mrs. Foster. Many of the local people used to work at 'Rudges', in Other Road fly dressing, or at Harris's rod making factory in Brittain Street, which later moved to Birchfield Road.

Along Birchfield Road there used to be a farm called Birch Tree Farm, run by three brothers called Rudge whose farm was next to a house called 'West End', which was situated on the corner of Musketts Way (20), opposite the house where David Thomas his brother, sister and mother and father lived. Proceeding along Birchfield Road towards Foxlydiate, one could see the Police Station, which was situated halfway between Langston's and what was Red Lane.

The Development of Webheath – Post 1950

The fifties were celebrated by wartime rationing coming to an end, although there were still many restrictions, especially on petrol. The King had died and Queen Elizabeth II ascended the throne. She was crowned in 1953 and to celebrate the occasion many street parties were held. On

---

62 Lily Norris, Old Redditch. p.97.

Tuesday 2nd June 1953, a party was held at Webheath Village Hall. The event was arranged by a committee, which had organized a lovely day. A short service was held at St. Philip's Church, then at mid-day there was a luncheon for older people, and in the afternoon there were sports going on – for all ages. Houses were decorated and judged and in the early evening there was a Fancy Dress Parade. The day finished off with a Social Evening in the Village Hall and a Bonfire at 11p.m. in Mr. Mill's field on the corner of Heathfield and Birchfield Road.

Much of the development of modern day Webheath has taken place over the last fifty years and in the 1950s most of the land which comprised the original heath was sold for development. Some of the land which belonged to Vincents Farm (now 183 Heathfield Road) and other properties which as we know formed part of the Plymouth Estate, were earmarked for development in the Draft Town Planning scheme of the 1950s. Mr. Drew, a local business man, bought some of the land for £700, but had to sell it back to Redditch Borough Council. Other portions of land belonging to the Plymouth Estate lying in Birchfield Road were also sold for development in 1946.

In January 1963, it was announced by Sir Keith Joseph, that Redditch should be a New Town, and in April 1964, after a public enquiry, it was designated as such. The next step was to establish the Redditch Development Corporation in order to plan the New Town. Various farms on the periphery of Redditch were compulsory purchased, to provide the land to build the houses needed. A Master Plan was designed including the infrastructure necessary for such an ambitious project. The Master Plan therefore proposed removing 'through' traffic from the Town Centre and basing the primary road network on a 'central box' of roads from which other primary routes radiated north-east, south-west. As part of these routes, some of the land belonging to Foxlydiate Farm was used to build part of the Bromsgrove Highway, which was opened in October 1979 (as already mentioned) by Mrs. Madge Guise, a long time resident of Webheath who had lived in Birchfield Road since 1934. Her family came from Foxlydiate, where her grandfather Mr. Lee ran the Post Office and Village Store there.

Other properties in Birchfield Road, as well as part of the original Redditch Golf Club, (in Plymouth Road) were demolished and also used to build part of the Highway. As a consequence of this Redditch Golf Club was re-located to its present site at Lower Grinsty in 1972.

In September 1984, the Town Centre Ringway was opened by Councillor Mrs. Joan Hadley, Chairman of the County Council and a member of the Board. Mr. & Mrs. Hadley restored and lived at Lower Grinsty Farmhouse in the mid 1970s until 1978. In 1989/90 other developments included the land at the back of Heathfield Road, originally part of Sycamore Farm, which now comprises Blackstitch Lane, Weatheroak and Yeadon Close. These houses were developed by Midland & General and Tarmac.

The next stage in the continuing development of Webheath, was the publication of the second Redditch Local Plan in the autumn of 1991. In amongst other considerations it was suggested that the area known as Norgrove should be considered for the provision of approximately 2000 dwellings. There were policies within the Local Plan which would provide a framework for development at Norgrove, with a Norgrove Development Brief to be prepared to outline the more detailed aspects. These included the provision for major roads, one of which could go through Morton Stanley Park.

As a result of these proposals an organization known as 'The South West Action Group' (SWAG) was formed to fight the proposed suggestions, under the Chairmanship of Bernard Atkins. The committee was composed of seven people, and within the organization, various sub-committees were formed, which covered such topics as Fund-raising, Technical, Publicity, and Liaison, all manned by a group of dedicated volunteers. Other groups were interested in the outcome of the Plan, such as Headless Cross Residents' Association, Bentley Parish Council and Bromsgrove District Council. All of whom would be affected in various ways by the impact of the development.

As a result of the objections put forward by the members of SWAG and other interested parties a Public Enquiry was held on 6th October 1992 in Redditch Town Hall. All the submissions for and against the plan were put forward and it was suggested by the Public Planning Inspector that a small development of 210 houses on a 20 acre site bounded by Church Road/Pumphouse Lane and the Borough boundary should be considered. The Inspector asked for the membership's reaction to this proposal. This was felt to be a form of compromise so the steering committee of SWAG recommended to their members that the proposal be accepted with two provisos: the Green Belt boundaries are firmly drawn and that sufficient facilities be available to meet the development envisaged. This was put to the members at a public meeting, where they voted to support the proposal.

The Inspector's Report went to the Planning and Transportation Committee in July/August 1993, but SWAG was reminded that there was no formal or legal obligation to accept the report and that unfortunately

Boxnott Farm.

was what happened. As a result of the objections received to the first, second and third Modifications, a second Public Enquiry was held on January/February 1995 with SWAG being called to object. This culminated in the fourth proposed Modifications to the Borough of Redditch Draft Local Plan No. 2 which were published in August 1995.

Amongst the Modifications proposed and accepted, were the Public Planning Inspector's original recommendations of 210 houses at a density of 10 dwellings per acre being situated off Church Road, Webheath. Also accepted were the modifications to the area of development restraint (ADR) which should include all of the land south of Pumphouse Lane and north of Crumpfields Lane. After an archaeological survey of the site in 1997 the development by David Wilson Homes took place and Boxnott Farmhouse was pulled down, with a large roundabout erected in its place.

One wonders how long this area described as Norgrove will remain free of development.

Webheath – like most other places has changed out of all recognition. It has always been inhabited, even though very sparsely during its life as a part of the Forest of Feckenham. With all its restrictions on land use; the land was still gradually cleared as well as being heathland and waste. We do not know much about the ordinary inhabitants, unless they had transgressed against forest laws, although they did have some rights. Most of the official records record those who had particular roles in the administration of the forest.

Webheath had a mainly agrarian economy until the 1800s, when the development of industry, mainly needlemaking encouraged people to move into the area. The rise in population was accelerated with the development of Redditch and its change into a New Town in 1964. Large parts of the Plymouth Estate were sold off which enabled more building to take place.

Population figures – Webheath
1841   792
1851   888
1861   823
1871   900
1901   1205[63]
1921   938 (Kelly's Directory 1928)

It is difficult to make a comparison of population changes, as the parish boundaries have changed, but, in 1991 Webheath and Headless Cross combined had a population of about 7,000 so Webheath would have roughly half that amount of people.

Parish boundaries changed as Redditch grew; from Webheath being a large area covering much of the ecclesiastical parish of Tardebigge, to the area it covers now. By a Confirmation Order of 1930, the greater portion of Webheath was transferred to the parish and Urban District of Redditch. By the County of Worcester Review Order 1933, the civil parish ceased to exist, part being transferred to the Urban District and parish of Redditch and the remainder to Tutnall and Cobley and Bentley Pauncefoot.[64] Modern Webheath seems to be designated as West Ward, part of Redditch Borough Council. Redditch Borough Council is divided into four County Council Divisions and twelve District Wards, as well as the one parish ward of Feckenham and Astwood Bank. At the last census of 2001, in West Ward, there were 5,461 persons living in an area of 344 hectares.[65] (For those of you who find acres easier to understand, the area covered is about 866 acres.)

A map of Webheath showing the areas developed post 1950 is included on the inside rear cover.

---

63 VCH Worcestershire Vol.IV pp.464-7.
64 Kelly's Directory of Worcestershire 1940. p.234.
65 Office for National Statistics.

Chapter 2

Various Groups and Activities Connected with Webheath

Sports and Pastimes

Although not strictly Webheath, Tardebigge Wake or Fair was held in the churchyard on the Sunday after St. Bartholomew's Day, but was discontinued sometime in the nineteenth century.[66] It was re-introduced and was held in various places, including Hewell Grange and the Vicarage Garden, which, when sold, the fair continued to be held on the first weekend in August in the church grounds. St. Philip's Church, the parish church of Webheath holds an annual fete.

Coursing

Hare coursing was a very popular rural pastime. Coursing meetings were held at Hewell, certainly before the First World War,[67] but it is not known when they were discontinued. Since the introduction of the Hunting Act of 2004, hare coursing is completely banned. With hare coursing there are usually one or two dogs and one hare. The dog is often a cross between a greyhound, saluki and a collie – a lurcher. These dogs competed against each other in a test of speed. The hares were made to run for their lives. The hare season ran from September 15th – March 10th.

Prize Fights

In his *Reminiscences of old Redditch* written in 1887, W. Avery, mentions the number of prize fights which used to take place in the vicinity. Sometimes people in anticipation of a "big mill" would collect a purse and get two

---

66 MD. p.99.
67 Berrow's Worcester Journal, November 1912.

men to fight for it, as was the case at Headless Cross when J. Millington and Tom Cook fought… at the old White Hart… which was a favourite resort of boxers. The taste for fighting spread to the inhabitants of the neighbourhood. Villages challenged each other. For instance Jack Chelly and Tom Watton came from Feckenham and challenged all comers.[68] It is understood that prize-fighting carried on into the twentieth century, as Mr. Mogg from Hunt End Farm was a well known local prize fighter.

When the canal was being constructed at Tardebigge, c.1811, there was a good deal of fighting with the navvies, who were wont to come over in the evening, and amuse themselves after their day's toil with fighting the Redditch men in the Pound Meadow.

'But the most Donneybrook (donney is S.E. Worcestershire dialect for hand) like affair that was ever seen, was once at Foxlydiate Wake, when a group of navvies came over to engage the chivalry of Redditch. Everyone was obliged to fight or run… From fists they came to sticks – it is said the navvies were provided with loaded ones. Palings were pulled up and a kid-pile being handy, all armed themselves and turned into Mr. Hemmings meadow (see article on Foxlydiate House), and fought until the navvies "cut their sticks" after having had serious if not fatal injuries inflicted on two of their "butties".' (A companion or friend.)[69]

Provision for Education

There was no school in Webheath originally, so children went to either Bentley, Headless Cross or Tardebigge. Even in the 1920s discussion took place on the advisability of an elementary school in Webheath, but as we know the schools were not built until the late 1950s/60s. In the 1940s/50s a village school was run in Webheath Village Hall, under the supervision of Mrs. Jarvis, who lived two doors away from the Hall. There was another teacher named Miss Notley. The school consisted of two classes – reception and infants – at each end of the room divided by a curtain and a stage. Ron Batson has fond memories of his schooldays, 'she was a splendid teacher'. Some of the children went on to Headless Cross School and then if they passed their eleven plus, to Redditch County High School. Redditch County High became a comprehensive and is now known as Trinity High School.

---

68 Alan Foxall. p.204.
69 Avery op. cit.

Now we have two First Schools in Downsell Road. Mount Carmel, built in 1968 and Webheath First School built in 1959. These schools were built as a result of school re-organisation in Worcestershire into a three tier system of First, Middle and Senior schools.

Webheath W.I.

This was formed in the 1950s. It started off with the founder members meeting in a private house in Crumpfields Lane until they found a more permanent meeting place. The group continued to meet for many years in the Village Hall, until it folded in c.2003 through lack of members.

In the back room of the Village Hall is an embroidered collage of Webheath 1976, made by members of Webheath Women's Institute, for the 50th anniversary of the opening of the Village Hall. Embroidered by:

Peggy Helme	Ruth Plim
Betty Scanlon	Sue Dutton
Beryl Weight	Betty Jarvie
Lorna Matthews	

Hewell Nursing Association

The Association was formed in 1894, to provide resident nurses at low fees to a body of regular subscribers, Lady Windsor being President and Hon. Treasurer and Mrs. Dickens (the Vicar's wife) being Hon. Secretary. Only one nurse was trained the first year, but later the Association embraced Bromsgrove, Finstall, the Lickey, Stoke Prior, Tardebigge and Wychbold. At one time sixteen regular and many extra nurses were employed.[70]

The White Heather Club

At some point in the middle '40s or '50s a social club was formed by local residents, who met in the schoolroom of the Village Hall. The members paid 6d. each to come to the meetings. In 1960, the W.V.S. (now W.R.V.S.) took over the running of the club and renamed it 'The White Heather Club'. Now, due to inflation and the rising cost of hiring the hall and paying for speakers, the charge is £1.

The club, nominally for senior citizens, although anyone would be welcome, is run by a committee who organise a varied afternoon of entertainments. The club meets each week on a Monday afternoon from 2p.m. – 4p.m. They organise a 'bring and buy' to raise funds for outings which the members can go on and during the afternoon, many people

---

70 MD. p.109.

come to give different talks or entertainment. Refreshments are provided by a group of volunteer tea ladies, after which the members enjoy a game of 'Bingo'. The afternoon is rounded off by singing a hymn. The number of members varies. In 2000 there were 68 members, but unfortunately due to various factors the numbers are down to 35. Lily Ashton, who is 91 years of age has been the Treasurer for seventeen years, and has been a member for 25 years. The present Leader is Joan McGovern.

The WRVS is one of the UK's largest volunteering organisations. The WRVS was initially formed during the Second World War to help civilians in their hour of need. It has 70 years experience of helping people in their local communities throughout England, Scotland and Wales. The volunteers and employees work together to support older people, giving practical help in all facets of their life.

The WRVS as part of their remit, operate social and lunch clubs for older people, as well as offering low cost meals to people living at home. Their service also operates help in hospital and mobile library services.

Horse Racing

Horse Racing was held on Webheath Common in the 1700s. Several notices appeared in a newspaper entitled *The Worcester Postman*, particularly in the period 1717/18/19.

> 'Friday July 4th 1718: A plate for £5 value to be run for upon Wib-Heath in the parish of Tardebigge upon Friday 11th inst. By any horse, mare or gelding carrying 10 stone, bridle and saddle included, nobody to ride any horse that ever won the value of one guinea. The best of three heats. The horse, mare or gelding that runs for this plate must be entered the same day they run, at the dwelling house of Thomas Dewce, known by the sign of the Fox and Goose in the parish of Tardebigge betwixt the hours of 6 and 9 in the morning, and to pay 2s 6d entrance each. The winning horse, mare or gelding to be sold for seven guineas.'[71]

Cock fighting

This was a very popular sport. 'A main of cocks' consisted of 12, 31, or 41 cocks exhibited by each of the interested parties. In major events birds had to weigh in the day before the event and the fights lasted two or three days.[72] In 1791 Lord Plymouth in letting land to John Moore obliged him to keep 'one dog and one cock' for the landlord's use in hunting and cock

---

71 Information Richard Churchley.
72 Gaut. p.142.

fighting. Lord Plymouth had a cock-pit near Barnt Green. Cock fighting, also carried on locally at the old White Hart where the cock-pit stood at the rear and side of the inn.[73] Cock fighting was banned in 1850.

Hunting

The Worcestershire Hunt was certainly in existence from the early 1700s, according to an inscription in Cotheridge churchyard, as well as a book of kennel accounts which was kept from 1733-1744 by Robert Berkeley Esq. Major Bland was the first recorded MFH, resigning in 1813 when Lord Foley succeeded him and started a subscription pack. Some distinguished Masters have served this Hunt, including Lord Coventry, before he established the Croome, the Marquess of Queensbury and the Earl of Dudley. More locally, Lt-Col. Gray-Cheape was Master 1951-1957. The kennels for the Hunt are situated at Fernhill Heath, Claines, Worcester. The country covered in Worcestershire is some thirty miles across, by twenty miles north to south. When the North Warwickshire ceased hunting in 1985, a new area between Redditch and Warwick was added. Packs of hunt dogs consist of Harriers, Beagles, Bassets and Foxhounds, but they are all separate hunts.[74]

The Royal British Legion

The British Legion was formed in 1921 as a move to solve the problems of the ex-Servicemen returning from the war. The four national organisations of ex-Servicemen which existed as a result of the Great War were amalgamated, and the title 'British Legion' was formally adopted in July 1921, with Earl Haig as its President.

The poppy emblem was initiated by an American nurse Moina Michael, a YWCA executive, who conceived the idea of wearing an artificial poppy in 1918 as a tribute to US veterans and to raise funds for disabled veterans. On 11th November 1921 the first British Poppy Day was held in Britain on the 3rd anniversary of the end of the Great War; the appeal raised £106,000. The work of raising funds continued, to make sure that returning servicemen from WWII were cared for and received a fair deal.

The Legion was granted a Royal Charter in 1925 in recognition of its work. On the Legion's 50th Anniversary in 1971, Her Majesty the Queen granted the 'British Legion' its 'Royal' prefix. In 1981 full membership was extended to serving members of Her Majesty's Forces.

---

73 Alan Foxall. p.204.
74 The Hunting Year Book, 2001/2.

Various branches were formed including those at Hewell, Redditch and Webheath. Hewell branch was formed after the Great War and when it disbanded its members went either to Bromsgrove or Webheath. Each branch was made up of ordinary members, associate members and a Women's Section, which organised many events to raise money for the various British Legion charities.

Webheath branch was founded after the Second World War on 11 September 1946. Two of the founder members were Harry Guise and Douglas Coates and the branch meetings were initially held at The Rose and Crown once a month on a Friday. Every Remembrance Day the Legion members would parade outside The Rose and Crown before marching down to St. Philip's Church. Unfortunately this practice came to an end in 1988, when the vicar of the time would not allow the members to sing 'Valiant Hearts'. After this their Remembrance Day Service was held in Webheath Village Hall.

The 'Tin House', which stood in Heathfield Road, was donated to The British Legion to be used as a club house by Mr. Tarleton a local builder, but planning permission was refused. (It is understood that the Tin House was made out of corrugated iron taken from a chapel. There was another Tin House situated at Hunt End.) However, Redditch Development Corporation were interested in the land and bought the site for £3,200.

In 1998 the branch decided to amalgamate with Redditch, due to falling numbers, but eventually the group carried on until around 2001, when there were only fourteen members. The branch was officially closed on 13th October 2005, by which time there were only 4-5 members. For a number of years the branch appears to have been dormant.[75]

In the entrance to Webheath Village Hall is a commemorative plaque to all members of the Webheath Branch of The Royal British Legion, both Men's and Women's Sections. The plaque is in remembrance of their past service to the village of Webheath.

"Lest We Forget"

---

75 Information County Secretary Royal British Legion.

Chapter 3

Local Charities

Parish of Tardebigge

The Whitbread Charity. Endymion Canning left £50 in his will dated 1631 for the poor, to be distributed by the Earl of Plymouth as he should think fit. After every Sunday Service portions of bread were distributed to the needy of Tardebigge. Two fourths to Redditch, one fourth to Webheath and Cur Lane and a similar portion to Bentley Pauncefoote.

Holyoakes Charity. In 1859 James Holyoake by his will bequeathed £2,000 for the benefit of the poor. The income in the early 1900s was distributed in blankets, sheets and other articles in kind to about seventy people. It is understood that certainly until the 1960s the recipients received blankets. Until recently, older people living in what was the Tardebigge side of Webheath, still received a basket of gifts or latterly, money, at Christmas time.

Social changes have outdated the original purpose of these charities. The Charity Commissioners have now agreed a new scheme to combine these two with the Charity of John Johnson founded in 1937 and the Queen Victoria Jubilee Fund (1897) in to two; to be known as Tardebigge Relief in Need Charity and Tardebigge Relief in Sickness Charity, to be administered by one set of Trustees comprising the three parish priests of Tardebigge, St. Stephen's in Redditch and Webheath – covering the old parish of Tardebigge, together with two representatives each from Tutnall and Cobley, Bentley Pauncefoot and Redditch Borough Council.

The trustees have agreed that the interest from the charities' investments shall henceforth be used to help people in need of all ages from the area. Modest amounts will be available and applications on behalf of individuals with genuine needs should be addressed to one of the clergy. (Tardebigge Parish Notes)

Parish of Feckenham

There were a variety of charities connected with the ancient parish of Feckenham (see Vol. III. p.119, VCH Worcestershire) which were amalgamated in 1907, under the title of the 'United Charities'. By this scheme the vicar was appointed an *ex officio* trustee to act with four representative trustees; one to be appointed by Redditch Borough Council and three to be appointed by the parish council of Feckenham. In the beginning the income from the charities was applied mainly in the distribution of bread and meat.

The charities were amalgamated c.1998, under one heading; to be called 'Feckenham Charity'; the income to be disposed of by the 'Trustee Body' as they think fit. At present the trustees consist of the Vicar, and three other trustees.

A notice is inserted in *The Feckenham News* to advise residents that funds are dispensed from this ancient charity to individuals and organisations within the boundaries of the ancient parish of Feckenham, as the Trustees think fit. Closing date for receipt of applications is 31st August of the current year.

Chapter 4

Some Place Names Connected with the District

BLACKSTITCH There is a field near Bordesley called Blackstitch. The element 'stitch' from *OE* meaning a bit, a portion, a ridge or allotment of land.

BOTTERS HILL (top of Green Lane). This name has long been of interest as to its origins, but in a book published by The Worcestershire Historical Society on *The Records of The Forest of Feckenham*, (pp.12, 164) the mystery may have been solved. In it there is reference in the middle 1240s to a William Le Bottere building a house and later, in the same publication in 1362 an Adam Bottare is mentioned as being a free tenant within the bounds of the forest. Since the name Botters Hill is shown as existing as early as 1591 on Blagrave's map, it is fairly safe to assume that the name is a personal one derived from those early inhabitants of the forest.

CURR LANE Also known as Crullelane, Corlond, Curlane. Could be a derivation of Crowle, *crull,* Old English 'curly' or, in a more general sense 'winding'. It described an area as well as a lane and probably covered the area beyond modern Webheath itself up to Tardebigge Church. There are records in the late fifteenth century of a forest court in which Cur Lane is mentioned, in Worcestershire Historical Society publication, *Miscellany One*, p.41.

DOWNSELL (Down hill) a wood on part of Lower Grinsty Farm, now part of the golf course. The wood was cut down during the Second World War.

GREEN LANE Its original meaning is self explanatory. It was the ancient thoroughfare to the church and village of Feckenham. However, the start of the lane, was originally called Botters Hill with all the fields adjacent to it having the prefix 'Botters', but, in 2003, the beginning of Green Lane (which used to join Heathfield Road) was re-named, and is now shown as being part of Crumpfields Lane. This change in emphasis was as a result of the development of Crumpfields Lane as a thoroughfare with the new road layouts, which occurred when the houses were built in Blackstitch Lane.

HENNALS Origin not known. First mentioned as 'Hynwelles' in 1516, belonging to a Robert Suarde. A one point connected with a mill called Hennals Mill, part of Lanehouse Farm.

HOCKING Gt. Hockings. Field name, derivation not precise, could mean 'a hump of ground'.

MUSKETTS WAY Originally Musquet Lane. (Itemised in the Enclosure Award for Tardebigge 1772.) Shown as Musketts Lane in 1840s.

SPRINGHILL self explanatory.

TYNSALL Tynsall Field was part of the original endowment of Bordesley Abbey. It was the ground between the old Alcester/Bromsgrove Road and the Lanehouse (now called Curr Lane) and Holyoakes Lanes.[76]

WEBHEATH Wibheath, Wybbheath. The family name of Webb is first mentioned in 1275 in connection with Tardebigge parish. The family gave its name to the farm in Copyolt Lane now called Tardebigge Farm. Webheath first appears in documents in the fifteenth century, usually in conjunction with Cur Lane; land we think which lay beyond the heath towards Tardebigge Church.

WOODEND CLOSE Takes its name from a house called 'Woodend' occupied by the Wright family. The house stood on the corner of Musketts Way.

---

76 MD. p.27.

Chapter 5

Notes and Jottings on Local Farms and Houses

Much of the early information on these properties is from various Census Returns, Tithe Award Maps, Kelly's Post Office Directories, Sale Particulars and various local Trade Directories. The dates relating to Kelly's are 1876, 1892, 1928, and 1940.

BIRCH TREE FARM Birchfield Road. Was situated on the edge of Pitcher Oak Wood. It is now the site of flats. In 1873 Thomas Hicks is listed as a dairy farmer. In 1920s-1960s the three Rudge brothers, Dick, Bob and Charles, farmed the land.

BOXNOTT FARM. In 1830s was bought by William Hemming[77] at which point was described as a small farm of about nine acres. In 1841 the owner is shown as George Silvestor, and tenant John Vincent farming approx. 83 acres. Andrew Hemming is listed in 1920, then Arthur G. Partridge from 1960s until sold. Boxnott Farm was only sold in the last few years and consists of a new development of housing of about 200 houses. As part of the remit for developing the site David Wilson Homes had to have an archaeological survey carried out in 1997.[78] The site archives are presently housed at Birmingham University Field Archaeology Unit. The survey showed remains of ridge and furrow, some of which can be seen in the field fronting onto Church Road in front of Holly Cottage. The evaluation of the site pointed to the possible remains of a rural medieval landscape as one would expect.

---

77 WRO BA5119.
78 C. Mould. HWCM 21776.

BROWNLAS FARM. Probably named after *Henry Brownless* who lived there in 1891. Brownlas Farm, situated in the lane by the side of Upper Norgrove was shown on the Tithe Award Map c.1840, originally owned by R. Hemming, then George Boulton Ladbury. In 1960s it was owned by Les Bryan. The original farmhouse is now a private house. Mr. Bryan built a bungalow by the side of the barn and sold off plots of land in Crumpfields Lane for development, possibly in the 60s.

CRUMPFIELDS FARM. Originally approx. 90 acres. The farmstead has a long history. The name may be derived from a family named Crumpe who lived in this vill in 1275.[79] The name 'Crumpfields' could also mean curved, crooked or sloping fields. It is shown on Blagrave's map of Feckenham (1591) as *Crowfield House.* There is also evidence of a possible moat on the farm. On Blagrave's Map the landholder was listed as Christopher Morgan.

By the early eighteenth century it was owned by John Boulton (will dated 1714), and continued to be farmed by members of the Boulton family, one of whom, Alice Boulton, married a Mr. Henry Waldron.[80] One of their children was named Robert Boulton Waldron (of Sillins). His son, also Robert Boulton Waldron, married Lucy Vernon of Hanbury Hall. As a widow, Lucy subsequently married Francis Haywood of Edge Lane Hall, Liverpool.

Crumpfields Farm had been bequeathed to Lucy Vernon (as she was) by Ann (d.1783) and Elizabeth (d.1781) Boulton. (I am indebted to Mr. C. Ginn for his information on the Boulton family.) As a result of which, Crumpfields Farm passed by marriage to Francis Haywood, (of Sillins), who subsequently rented the farm to other members of the Boulton family. In 1851 it was rented by William Boulton, and his son, Edwin Francis Boulton.[81]

In 1912 the Sillins Estate (of which Crumpfields was a part) was sold. The farm appears to have been bought by Mr. S. French for £2,350. (Estate particulars) Mr. French sold it 1918, the tenant at the time being a Mr. W.E. Hillman. Farmed 1920 Colver. In 1928 part of the farm was farmed by John Cresswell. By 1940 farmed by the Hims family. (Mrs. Mary Hims).

The present owners of part of the farm are Mr. and Mrs. W. Finney. Mrs. Finney's maiden name was Christine Hims. Her father, Thomas Henry Hims was the son of Mary Hims and her husband Levi Hims, who was a needle manufacturer.

---

79 EPNS Worcestershire.
80 WRO BA351 705: 81p4b.
81 Census Feckenham, 1851.

In the 1930s and 40s the farm ran a herd of Ayrshire cows and was run by Thomas Henry Hims and his mother Mary, who died in 1943. The farming Hims of Crumpfields had a milk round and after hand milking the cows, Mrs. Hims washed and filled the bottles ready for delivery to the Redditch area and after delivering the milk from a Morris van, the milking process was recommenced in the late afternoon. However, despite the long hours and hard work, wartime restrictions meant that the farm could not produce enough milk to supply its customers and so the milk round was sold to Quinney's Dairy at Crabbs Cross.

Millie Hims had a few sheep which she treated as pets, but these sheep produced several sets of triplets, even quads, prompting the *Redditch Indicator* to publish an article recording the fact.

Like many other local children, Christine went to school at Bentley Pauncefoot, walking across the fields each day. Eventually she went to Hill Court School, becoming the school's first ever head girl. After school Christine trained as a secretary and went to work at Abel Morall, where she met and married her husband, Bill, who also worked at Abel Morall as a tool maker.

Crumpfields Farmhouse has been sub-divided over the years between families, but the farmhouse part that is occupied by Christine and Bill Finney has recently gone through extensive restoration and is now a cosy and warm farmstead. For some time Muriel Tongue (née Hims) and her husband Harold Lionel looked after part of the farm with son David as well as Pumphouse Farm.

The Tongue family were prosecuted in August 1995 for failing to look after their animals, and were fined. They appeared before magistrates again in December 1996 for having twice as many cows on the two farms than they were designed to hold. The three farmers appealed against a ban for keeping livestock in April 1997 and had to pay another fine.

They did not appear to have learnt their lesson as in October 2002 they were prosecuted again and banned from keeping animals for life for causing unnecessary suffering to livestock at six farms in the Redditch area. Despite the life ban the brothers David and Steven Tongue and their father Harold breached the court order in April 2003. As a result of which in May 2003, David was sentenced to 12 weeks in jail, while Steven was sentenced to 6 weeks in prison. Harold was sentenced to three months' custody, suspended for two years.

The Tongues, who own farms in Webheath, Rowney Green, Rous Lench, and Inkberrow, were also each ordered to pay £2,500, in costs. (They finally left Crumpfields Farm in 2005.) The case against the

Tongues continued; as they were jailed in May 2006 for twelve months each for failing to pay the fines which were handed out to them in 2003. Their cattle which were being left to fend for themselves on the farm in Rowney Green were in such bad condition that 90 had to be destroyed. The police seized the animals and put them in the care of the RSPCA. Eventually circa September 2006, the cattle were moved to an undisclosed destination where they could be properly managed and their welfare needs properly met.[82]

Extracted from reports in the *Redditch Advertiser* August 1995, December 1996, April 1997, November 2002, May 2003, February 2004, *The Standard* August 2006, *The Advertiser* August 2006, September 2006.

FOXLYDIATE FARM. (I am indebted to Mr. Fred Shrimpton for the following information.) Mr. Fred Shrimpton comes from a long established Redditch family who moved from Long Crendon in 1861 and set up a building and contractors firm in Mount Pleasant.

Mr. Shrimpton who is 86 years old, grew up in Rectory Road, Headless Cross. He was demobbed after the Second World War in 1946, and then went to live in Mount Pleasant. Foxlydiate Farm was bought by the Shrimpton family c.1947 from the Bentley Estate. The previous tenant was Mr. Richard Hughes and his two sons, who went to live in Hill Cottage on Birchfield Road. Mr. Hughes was 96 years old when he died. The farmhouse had been empty for about four years, but the dairy farm had been run by the family since its purchase. Mr. and Mrs. Shrimpton moved into the farmhouse in 1951 and ran the farm as well as having a building and contractors business, which subsidised the farm. The dairy side of the farm was run by the family until 1958, after which the dairy buildings were modernised. Mr. Shrimpton used to rear calves for the beef trade and also reared store cattle. At some time they also had poultry with a few fields used for growing crops for food and hay for the cattle and winter fodder. The animals were taken to various markets, the earliest being at Barnt Green next to the station. Other markets used were Bromsgrove and Kidderminster cattle markets; Mr. Shrimpton also bought calves from Worcester.

The field in which Hennalls Avenue is situated was purchased, by Redditch Borough Council in the 1950s. Some of the farmland opposite to the farm was designated by the Development Corporation to be used

---

82 Extracted from reports in the Redditch Advertiser, August 1995, December 1996, April 1997, November 2002, May 2003, February 2004. The Redditch Standard, August 2006, The Advertiser, August 2006, September 2006.

to build the Bromsgrove Highway, which was opened in October 1979 by Mrs. Madge Guise. Part of the farm (10 acres) was sold to Bryants in 1985 for development i.e. Reynards Close.

Mr. Shrimpton who lost his wife in 1982, has been a staunch member of the congregation at Tardebigge Church for over fifty years. He has been Churchwarden twice, sung in the choir for fifty years and is currently the Sexton. Foxlydiate Farm was sold in August 1987, with Mr. Shrimpton reserving 20 acres of the land.

Foxlydiate House. Was situated at the top of Foxlydiate. It was built by Edgar Sealey. But was sold and pulled down, the land used for development.

FOXLYDIATE HOUSE. (The original house) stood where the present Foxlydiate Hotel stands. Built by William Hemming, who was a needle manufacturer in Beoley Lane. He was the same William Hemming mentioned by William Avery in connection with the various strikes that were held by the needle Pointers in 1846 when conditions and prices were laid down by the Needle Manufacturers. A circular was published stating the prices to be paid by the various proprietors and signed by William Hemming, Chairman.

The house must have been built in the 1830/40s as it is clearly shown on the Tithe Award Map. It was a very substantial property, consisting of a house and garden, arable, common and pasture land, of about 173 acres. In addition to which he also owned the Fox and Goose Public House. By 1851 the property had been sold or was occupied by Robert Henry Johnson Esq. In 1873 it was 'the seat' of John Doherty, Esq., (registrar of HM court of probate for the County of Warwick.)

In 1908 was occupied by Mortimer Margesson, and then from 1914-20s was occupied by Mrs. V. Milward.

It was listed in 1910 (Needle District Almanack) as being occupied by Mr. McCandlish. There seems to have been a gap in him residing there as there is reference to him living in Bromsgrove; then he resided there again in the 1930s when it was sold c.1935.

William McCandlish lived in or owned Foxlydiate House from c.1908 to c.1935 when it was put up for sale. He played a prominent part in the history of the Bromsgrove Guild after he became a partner in the company in 1906. When the Bromsgrove Guild became a limited company, William McCandlish was one of the chief shareholders. He was involved with running the company for most of his life until he died in 1947. He had moved from Worcestershire to Hampshire in 1935 because of his wife's poor health, but continued his connection with the company and regularly travelled up to Bromsgrove from the country.

The Bromsgrove Guild's most important commission, were the ornamental gates in front of Buckingham Palace. There is a complete list of the Guild's accomplishments included in a book about the Guild, entitled *The Bromsgrove Guild* edited by Quentin Watt; however, some of the local examples include the Calvary Cross in the churchyard in Feckenham; with some of their most famous examples shown in the church of the Holy Trinity and St. Mary Dodford.

FOXLYDIATE HOTEL was built in 1939 by Epsley's of Evesham on the site of Foxlydiate House. It was opened by the well known actress Evelyn Laye. The licence from the old Fox and Goose was transferred to the new hotel and The Fox and Goose was pulled down. Many local social events have been held at the hotel, including the Annual Christmas Dance for the Redditch Cricket, Hockey and Rugby Club.

THE GABLES was owned by G. Leach JP. Originally situated in Birchfield Road by the side of the footpath, Musketts Way where the highway is now. (It was considered as a clubhouse for the original Redditch Golf Cub.) At one point it was a nursing/maternity home.

HIGH HOUSE FARM. Is listed in 1844 – 117 acres, the tenant at the time was a William Bradley. High House Farm was sold c.1951 by F.J. Coney, when it was described as 'having an excellent modernised farmhouse, all modern farm buildings, with I.C.I. grass drying plant, 2 capital cottages and 214 acres, 3 roods 14 perches of pasture, arable land and woodland, and a large brewhouse.' High House Farm won the President's Cup for the best cultivated farm over 120 acres in the Bromsgrove and District Farmer's Club 1951.

In c.1964 it was recorded in the *Indicator* that 'a 56 year old woman died in a blaze at High House Farm, Tardebigge early one Sunday morning. She was named Eileen Foyle who was alone in the house at the time. The fire was discovered shortly after 6a.m. By Mr. John Ingram a farm worker who was employed working on the farm. He tried to enter the house but, when he was unable to do so called the fire brigade.

Firemen broke into the house using breathing apparatus and put out the blaze which had taken a hold mainly in an upstairs bedroom and had started to spread downwards…

Mrs. Foyle was the wife of John Foyle, joint Managing Director of Boxfoldia Ltd. Birmingham. Their only daughter is married and living in San Francisco. At that time High House Farm was the property of Boxfoldia Ltd.'

HILL FARM First mentioned in seventeenth century as being in the occupation of a Mr. D'Abitot. It was converted into two cottages many years ago, which were known as Tack Cottages. In 1958 both cottages were unoccupied and had been vandalised. They were offered to Mr. & Mrs. David Thomas by Dr. Houfton. The cottages were demolished and Hunters Hill was built on the site by Harrison Bros. of Redditch.

HOLBORNE FARM No.161 on Tithe Award Map. Used as a saw mill by the Pollards and is now owned by David Partridge and Son.

LANE HOUSE FARM. The 1851 Census shows the farm as approx. 155 acres, farmed by Richard Cotterell.

The following information was kindly supplied by Ron Tongue who was born 21st December 1916.

The Tongue family farmed the farm for three generations. Ron's grandfather was the first tenant followed by Ron's father and a brother who took over the farm. During the 1940s Ron took over the tenancy of the farm. When Ron left Tardebigge Village School at the age of fourteen he went to work as an apprentice carpenter on the Hewell Estate for the princely sum of 2/-6d. a week. He continued in this job until he went to work with his father on the farm.

Lanehouse was a mixed farm of about 200 acres. Everything was grown – corn, rye, etc. while they had sheep, cattle and poultry. During the war much of the land was ploughed up to grow wheat – about 100 acres. In those days harvesting was all done by a binder and then put into sheaves and stooks. The binder twined the corn into sheaves and there were six sheaves in a stook. They were taken by harvest wagons and stored in a barn or built into ricks. In the winter they hired a threshing machine in the barn or if the weather was right out in the open. One shute went into a sack which weighed about 100cwt. and had to be carried on the farmer's back to a top granary. The straw was then made into trusses before it went into a baler, which fed wires round the straw into bales. The farmer then twisted the wire with his thumb and finger, which made the fingers very sore. The bales also weighed about 100cwt. each. These were also made into ricks.

As one approaches Lanehouse Farm from Webheath one goes down the hill to a stream, part of which was known as 'the Sheepwash'. It was used by the local farmers to wash the sheep and had proper, brick built sluices. In the summer all the lads went swimming, paddling or fishing there. It was also a general meeting place.

On the Webheath side of the stream a pumping station was built in about 1974 using water obtained from a borehole which was about 21 ins. in diameter. The water feeds the population of Redditch. The ground was boggy and not much use for farming so the Water Board put the pumping station there. The borehole goes through various strata of rock, one of which contained the footprint of a giant tiger, another was agate while another contained sea weed. The farm had a climax windmill which supplied them with water.

From the Sheepwash is a footpath now covered over but was originally made of cobbles. This path led down to a cottage called Hennalls Mill. It had not functioned as a mill for many years and was used as a labourers cottage for the Lanehouse Farm. Around the mill was a very elaborate embankment, probably to do with the mill when it was used to grind corn. When the tenant moved out it lay derelict for some years. It was not used as it had been assumed there was no road to the Mill, although in fact the lane had become covered by grass. The lane continued on past the cottage to a gate which was used by the Countess Plymouth. The cottage was used for target practice during the Second World War, first by The Home Guard who knocked it about, until the Army came along and demolished it with mortar fire.

In the 1940s the Plymouth estate was sold to cover death duties. The farmers all went to various meetings at Dr. Houftons's Surgery and at the solicitors at Astwood Bank, on the understanding that they would be given the opportunity to buy their individual farms. But in the meantime a consortium of farmers had got together to buy most of the estate, so the farmers had to buy their farms from them.

Lanehouse Farm was valued at £4,750. The actual acreage was given as 181.941 acres and was bought by Mr. H. Tongue. It was subsequently sold to the Bentley Estate.

MARLPIT FARM Owned by Harry Smith c.1930. Ray Harper also ran the farm and had a milk round.

OXSTALLS FARM. Salters Lane (opposite wood in Salters Lane). Originally part of the Plymouth Estate and sometimes Tack Farm, or Birchensale Farm.

PUMPHOUSE FARM Originally part of the Plymouth Estate and served as the Tardebigge Workhouse until 1834. It was occupied in 1844 by John Callow and consisted of a house and garden and three fields, totalling about 20 acres. In 1851 John Parker farmed the property which was by then 60 acres, and employed one labourer. A street directory of 1920 listed a Henry Bartlam, which is the Mr. Bartland mentioned by H. Rider Haggard. Now owned by Steven and David Tongue. Incorporated into the farm buildings is The Schoolroom.

SHELTWOOD FARM. The original manor of Sheltwood was granted to Bordesley Abbey by Empress Maud. The estate remained in the possession of the abbey until the Dissolution. By 1571 it had passed to Edward Lord Windsor. In 1599 Henry Cookes of Sheltwood was a churchwarden. In 1650 it was placed under Cur Lane. Until 1864 a Tithe Barn stood where the two Sheltwood Cottages now stand, called Tithe Barn Cottages, when Lady Windsor re-built many of the estate cottages. In 1770 – farmed by John Shelton (rent roll). In 1851 was approximately 300 acres, farmed by Joseph Brown, a Mrs. Buckley 1920. In 1940 A.G. Brazier. (See Monica Dickens pp.5, 7, 8, 20, 27). There are also many references to the manor in *Records of Feckenham Forest 1236-1377*.

SPRING HILL FARM FOXLYDIATE. In 1838 it was farmed by John Callow. It was reported in the *Worcester Herald* of May 1838 that the residence of Mr. J. Callow was broken into and about 800lbs. of bacon, ham, etc. were stolen. The robbers effected an entrance by forcing the iron bars of the kitchen window, in which rooms the hams were placed. It is supposed that three men at least must have been in the house and although a particularly savage pointer bitch was in the kitchen with two other dogs in the house, not the slightest alarm was given. A circumstance which leads to the supposition that the robbers were parties to whom the dogs were familiar. A liberal reward has been offered for the discovery of the offenders, but nothing has transpired to fix the guilt on anyone, nor has any trace of the property been discovered. It consisted of approx. 110 acres. By 1851 farmed by William Rudge. Thomas Henry White farmer and wholesale butcher 1873.

By the 1930s was farmed by Mr. H. Hill who was a prominent member of the local community. As Ruby Gardner mentions in her memoirs, Howard Hill's son had a butchers shop in Market Place in 1920s and, in the summer the family used to hold pageants in the farm grounds. It was farmed by R. Farmer in 1940s/60s and was also a boarding house. (Kelly's Directory 1940). D. J. Farmer in 1963. Afterwards Mr. Tracy.

SPRINGHILL HOUSE. 269 Birchfield Road. Was originally a farm which was sold by Cross and Harris. At one point a Sidney Smith lived there. Mr. Smith had a factory down Beoley Road making Sail palms for mending ships. His wife, Millie, was a keen golfer.

It was sold c.1967 for over £15,000. It was a substantial house, which was originally the farmhouse for a dairy farm. In 1911 it was described as 'Freehold or Dairy Pleasure Farm situate in Webheath near the town of Redditch, comprising a well built farm house and farm buildings containing about 24 acres. The farm buildings, which are well built and conveniently arranged around a walled-in yard, comprise Cow Shedding to tie 24 Cows, stable for Two Horses, Chaff House, Two large Lofts, Coach House, Four Pig Styes and Cistern. A large fruit orchard and well maintained Pasture Land. (Sale Particulars) Owner Mr. Hunt, decd.' It was subsequently pulled down and the site now has six houses on it.

SPRINGVALE COTTAGES lived in by the Bayliss (Rhona Bayliss née Harris) and Harwood families. Harwood went to keep the post office at Foxlydiate. Mr. Hands developed the post office and the two houses between the Post Office and Hill Cottage. The gardens to the cottages now have houses situated on them.

SPRINGVALE HOUSE occupied in 1873 by Mrs. Anne Wykes. Occupied by Howard Lee 1920. It was lived in by Mr. and Mrs. Baker from 1961- 2001. It was originally owned by the Gray-Cheape family of Bentley Manor, occupied by Mr. Newby. The house was bought at auction at Foxlydiate and sold by Banks and Silvers for £4,000. Mr. and Mrs. Baker came from Windsor, but moved from there for Mr. Baker to run the Electrical Department at H.D.A. (Notes given by Mrs. Baker). By the side of Springvale House was an orchard and a spinney with a brook which runs across to Springhill Farm. They have now been developed, with houses erected on them.

SYCAMORE FARM sometimes known as Hill Top, farmed in 1851 by John Tipping 80 acres. In 1912 the farm was sold as part of the Sillins Estate. The tenant at the time was Mr. Jackson. A. Cook farmed the land in 1920. Much of Sycamore Farm now forms part of the Redditch Golf Club, as well as the development in Blackstitch Lane. In the 1940s was owned/tenanted by Mr. Turner. He had a German POW working on the farm called Hans, who Ron Batson comments, would weigh them as children, on the weighing machine when he was weighing the potatoes.

TACK FARM. Originally named Quarry Farm[83] was a farm of approx. 338 acres. (1851) Walter Walford was the farmer employing seven labourers. In the 1920s the tenant was C. J. Owen. Dr. Houfton took over the tenancy of the farm at the beginning of the war in 1940. He continued as a doctor and surgeon at Redditch and lived next to his surgery in Worcester Road. He purchased the farm when the Plymouth Estate was sold in 1946 and went to live at Tack Farm after the house had been renovated. The farm was bought in 1966, by a farmer known as Jones the Pig. His son subsequently killed his mother at the farmhouse. The farm was well known for its herd of Jersey Cows. When the Bromsgrove Highway was built it was excavated 30 feet below the old road to help obviate the noise of the traffic.

THATCHED COTTAGE lived in for some time by Mr. Dyde and his mother. Also a Mr. and Mrs. Long. (Note Mrs. Baker)

UPPER NORGROVE Originally the estate office for the Bentley Estate, run by H. Thornton Jagger in the early 1900s. Miss W. E. Compton lived there in 1930s. Owned in 1963 by Mr. & Mrs. L. Ludford. At some point in time it became a kennels. Run as a young offenders unit, now single flats.

WOODEND a house owned by a Mr. Wright which stood on the corner of Musketts Way. 'The Gables' stood on the other corner. Wood End Close takes its name from the original house.

WESTCROFT. Was built for Sydney Huins. Sold to Mr. Schofield for £5,300 then to Richard Thomas Solicitor. Was sold to Redditch Development Corporation. It is now a kindergarden.

WOODLAND STORES The Woodland Stores was a separate development – the land was originally part of Foxlydiate House – which was pulled down and is now The Foxlydiate Hotel. The store was probably built in 1930s. It was run as a general stores in 1950s by Miss Harvey. People used to walk to the Woodland Stores for a cup of tea and refreshments. In 70s/80s, it was run as a butchers shop by Mick Blundell. It has now been demolished.

Rhona Bayliss (née Harris) – who worked in The Woodland Stores and lived in the cottages called Springhill Cottages disturbed an intruder who broke into her cottage – she threatened him with a shot gun. Her husband worked on Birchensale Farm.

---

83 MD. p.27.

Chapter 6

Webheath Landowners

The Haywood Family

The Waldron Haywood family had been resident at 'Sillins' for about 250 years. It was originally owned by the Boulton family and passed through marriage to Robert Waldron. Robert Waldron had a son John, two daughters and another son, named Robert Boulton Waldron. His son, also named Robert Boulton Waldron, married Lucy Vernon of Hanbury Hall and they had a daughter who died in infancy. Robert Boulton Waldron died in 1823, after which Lucy, his widow, married Francis Haywood of Liverpool in 1826. They had three children. Two sons; Edward Waldron Haywood and Russell Haywood, and a daughter, Lucy.

Lucy Haywood née Vernon died on Jan 9th 1871 at 'Sillins' aged 71 years. When she died her estate passed to Edward.

Edward Waldron Haywood was a person of some importance and there are many memorials to the family in Feckenham Church. He was a local J.P. and Deputy Lieutenant of Worcestershire. Edward married Ada Hislop of Hindlip Hall. The Haywoods were friends with all the local gentry, sharing a passion for hunting. The Squire of Bentley – Mrs. Cheape, was one of their particular friends.

The Haywoods did not have any children and when Edward died in 1908 his sister Lucy, who superseded her elder brother (Russell had already died) must have inherited the estate, which was put up for auction in 1912.

The estate was sold in lots to a variety of people, raising a large amount of money. The amount raised being in the region of £25,000. The house passed through various hands including Mr. and Mrs. Ellis. Mrs. Ellis was Mrs. Cheape's daughter.

During the war it was commandeered for use by the War Office. The American Army were billeted there to begin with and afterwards it was a prisoner of war camp; first for German Prisoners of War and then for Italians.

(From original research by Elizabeth Atkins.)

The Hemming Family

The Hemmings were an old Warwickshire family who originally resided at the Manor House, Great Alne. The original Richard Hemming carried on the manufacture of needles in Great Alne, but as the trade increased a warehouse was erected at Redditch, possibly in Beoley Lane. (Bentley's Directory of 1840, lists W. Hemming needle manufacturer in Beoley Lane.) Richard Hemming and Sons are listed in 1840 under Tardebigge and Redditch as manufacturers of needles.[84] Richard Senior's two sons, William and Richard carried on the family business. Property was acquired at Prospect Hill, and after the old squire died, Richard Junior lived on at the Manor House whilst William went to reside at Prospect Hill and take over the running of the needle making business.[85]

Richard Hemming (Senior) must have been established before 1800 as Monica Dickens in her book *A Thousand Years in Tardebigge*, records that in 1781 Sarah Hemming wife of Richard Hemming of Redditch, needlemaker, bought three houses, 'at or near the gate at Foxlydiate'. In 1812 Richard Hemming, Esq., was in possession of three houses detached and bordering the road where the old Foxlydiate House stood. By 1840 William Hemming had built Foxlydiate House, on the site of these houses, (he must have acquired the property from his father) as well as acquiring more land at Foxlydiate.[86] Shortly after 1838 Mr. Thomas Cookes sold the Bentley estate to William Hemming of Foxlydiate.[87] Mr. W. Hemming greatly enlarged the house at Bentley, known originally as Bentley Lodge House – or known locally as Pigeon House, and called it Bentley Manor. The original Bentley Manor House is now Bentley Manor Farm.

William Hemming was a very important member of the needle manufacturing fraternity. During his lifetime he was High Sheriff of Worcestershire in 1846 and had married a daughter of Humphrey Chamberlain, head of the Worcestershire China Works. He was described by Joseph Bentley in his History of Worcestershire c.1840 as 'one of the oldest and most respected needle manufacturers in the country'. His

---

84 Bentley Directory, 1840.
85 M. Ellis, The Squire of Bentley.
86 Tithe Award Tardebigge.
87 MD p.158.

description of the process of needlemaking has been used in the main body of the history of Webheath.

In September 1846 the Needle Pointers in the vicinity went on strike for more money. As a result of which the needle manufacturers under the chairmanship of William Hemming met to discuss and fix the list of prices for pointing the needles and fish hooks mentioned in the said list. They agreed that all of them should abide by the prices set. This was agreed upon by all fifty-four manufacturers, based in the surrounding villages of Feckenham, Studley, Alcester and its vicinity. Although the strike continued it did not last longer than November of the same year when the Pointers accepted the Master's terms, broke up their union and commenced work again.[88]

William Hemming had two sons, Walter and Richard. It is assumed that they resided at Foxlydiate until they married. Walter Chamberlain Hemming is listed as Lord of the Manor of Bentley, at Bentley Lodge in 1851, while Richard, 'R.H.' as he was known, lived at Bordesley Hall. After William's death in 1848, 'R.H.' became possessor of both Bentley and Foxlydiate and took over the sole partnership of the business.[89] 'R.H.' became High Sheriff of Worcestershire in 1863, following in his father's footsteps, who had been High Sheriff in 1846.[90] The holdings of Richard 'RH' Hemming in 1873 amounted to 2,486 acres. (Landowners in 1873) In the same list a Walter C. Hemming of Bewdley is listed as holding over 1,000 acres.

The needle and fish hook manufactories of Richard Hemming and Son, were based at Prospect Hill and Forge Mills, Bordesley. They are listed in various Post Office Directories, as being based at Prospect Hill certainly until 1940, although Richard 'R.H.' had died in 1891. Forge Mill at Bordesley was leased from the Plymouth estate and was sold c.1947, to defray death duties when the Earl of Plymouth died.

Both branches of the Hemmings passed into the female line. Richard Hemming's youngest daughter, Favoretta (Mrs. Walter Ingram) was left the business in Redditch, while his eldest daughter Maude (Mrs. M. Cheape) was left the whole of his landed estates, including Bentley, in England and Scotland on the death of her father in 1891.[91] Maude, had married Lt.-Col. G. Cheape in 1873. Lt.-Col. Cheape died in 1900. 'The Squire of Bentley' as she was known, died November 1919.

---

88 William Avery, Old Redditch, 1888.
89 M. Ellis op. cit. p.21.
90 Ibid. pp.29/30.
91 Ibid. p.183.

The Plymouth Family – Hewell Grange

The Earl of Plymouth was the major local landowner until the mid-1940s when the estate was sold to cover death duties.

The Windsors of Hewell have a long and illustrious history. The barony of Windsor was created in 1529, while their ownership of the manor of Stanwell, in Middlesex, can be traced back to the Norman Conquest. Unfortunately in 1542, Lord Windsor was compelled to accept the Abbey of Bordesley, Worcestershire and other lands in exchange for the lands at Stanwell. The Abbey of Bordesley was situated in the parish of Tardebigge, where the Windsors were to make their new home. This was situated at Hewell Grange, the principal grange of the former Abbey.

By the beginning of the nineteenth century an earldom had been created, which passed to Other Archer, who became the sixth earl. One of his sisters, Harriet, married the Hon. Henry Clive (Lord Clive of India's grandson). When the sixth earl died the barony of Windsor fell into abeyance between his two sisters, one of whom as mentioned was Lady Harriet Clive. The earldom passed to two uncles, both of whom died without issue and the Earldom of Plymouth consequently became extinct.

The Hon. Robert Henry and Lady Harriet Clive had six children, the eldest of whom was Robert Clive, born in 1824. The Hon. Robert Henry Clive died in 1854 and his widow had the abeyance of the Barony of Windsor terminated in her favour and took the name of Windsor (in addition to and before that of Clive).

Their son Robert Clive (afterwards Windsor-Clive) married Lady Mary Bridgman in 1852. They had four children: Robert George and three daughters.

Robert George Windsor-Clive was born in 1857 and inherited the barony of Windsor in 1869 on the death of his grandmother Lady Harriet. He inherited the Windsor estates at the age of twenty-one on 27th August 1878 and his coming of age was celebrated in all the parishes that comprised the Windsor estates. He became Lord of the Manors of Bromsgrove and Tardebigge.

A succession of shrewd alliances had enlarged the landholdings of the Windsor family. By 1873, the family's possessions included large tracts of land in Wales, Shropshire and Worcestershire. In 1873 for example, Lord Windsor is listed as being the fourth largest landowner in Worcestershire with 8,519 acres of land worth £13,080 a year. In Worcestershire the estate was situated mainly in the parish of Tardebigge, with the house at Hewell Grange. The estate included most of Tardebigge, including much of Webheath, the rapidly growing town of Redditch, as well as land at the Lickeys, Barnt Green, Alvechurch and Cofton Hackett.

As well as running their estates, Lord Windsor was part of the Government; as Paymaster General under Lord Salisbury (1891-2) and Chief Commissioner for Works (1902-5) under A.J. Balfour. One of his forebears, the fifth Earl of Plymouth, Other Hickman, was Chairman of Worcestershire Quarter Sessions during his lifetime, while Robert George Lord Windsor (Earl of Plymouth by 1905) was on the Commission for Peace for the County of Worcestershire.[92]

In the early twentieth century the Windsor family were very involved in the social and economic life of Tardebigge. Tardebigge Village Hall was built by the Earl of Plymouth in 1911 (now 'The Tardebigge') for the use of the local parishioners, who had to pay a small yearly subscription. This was the centre for many events, of which the people from Webheath must have been able to participate. In fact Webheath Parish Council sometimes used the village hall for their meetings.

Lady Windsor was involved with many good works. Her social life was balanced by the duties of a country landowner. Her concern for the well-being of the tenants at Hewell took the practical form of providing courses in which useful country skills were taught. The traditional craft of quilting was revived, weaving tweed provided a prosperous sideline and all manner of artistic crafts were encouraged and taught.[93]

Lord Windsor was a sporting man. He was a good shot, a keen golfer and supporter of many sports. In Worcestershire he supported many of the local sports including cricket, and provided club facilities for Barnt Green Cricket Club as well as the ground at Hewell, which was situated in the lane on the way to the Old Wharf. He provided the land for the Bowling Club and was its President.

Robert George died in March 1923 and was succeeded by his son Ivor Miles who died in October 1943. The estate was sold in 1946/7 to defray death duties.

---

92 Elizabeth Atkins. Unpublished thesis M.A. University of B'ham 1995, p.10.
93 Ibid. p.38.

Glossary

Alienate – to transfer property.

Assarts – a piece of woodland which has been cleared, enclosed and converted into arable land.

Boards of Guardians – were set up after the Poor Law act of 1834, to be in charge of the administration of the relief of the poor.

Bailiwick – an area under the jurisdiction of a bailiff, or, in the case of the forest the forester in fee.

Common – land in a manor which is there for the use of the people – the right of people to pasture their cattle on the common.

Conterminous – having a common boundary.

Copyhold – land held by a copy of the title on the court rolls. Copyhold tenure was abolished in 1922.

Encroach – to trespass or settle on land which is not theirs. Very often on land which was waste at the side of a road.

Forest – an expanse of land designated as an area for hunting. It covered not just woods, but villages and cultivated land, and the people living in these areas would be subject to the laws of the forest, which could be very harsh.

Hams – a piece of enclosed land, by a river.

Headborough – in Anglo-Saxon times each vill was divided into tithings or ten households and the headborough was their representative. Also later on another term for a constable.

Lay Subsidy Roll – list of taxes paid on a person's moveable goods. Written on a roll of parchment.

Liberty – an area situated outside a borough in which freemen had certain rights of pasture, also an area in which the Lord of the Manor had certain privileges.

Manor – a unit of organisation. It was an estate held by a landlord (not necessarily a titled person). A manor could be part of a parish, contiguous with its boundaries, or spread over more than one parish. The Lord of the Manor retained part of the land for his use and the rest was tenanted or else used for commons or waste.

Overseers of the Poor – at least two persons who were appointed yearly by the vestry, subject to approval by the Justices of the Peace. They levied the poor rate and supervised its distribution.

Perches – when standardised measured 16½ feet. Also known as a rod or a pole.

Poles – see perches

Rods – see perches

Roods – when standardized a measure of 40sq. rods. One acre = 4 roods.

Township – a division of a parish which formed a unit of administration; it levied a Poor Rate and appointed a constable.

Settlement – Settlement Act of 1697. Strangers were allowed to settle in a new parish if they were armed with a certificate from their home parish, guaranteeing they would take them back if they needed assistance.

Union – A combination of parishes formed to administer poor relief and build workhouses.

Vill – a division of a Parish, may be synonymous with township.

Vestry The – in the past, the governing body of a parish.

Waste – communal land used by tenants of a manor, very often on manor boundaries or on the edges of roads.

Bibliography

Atkins Elizabeth *An Aristocratic Family in the late Nineteenth Century* (MA University of Birmingham 1995).

Avery William *Old Redditch: being an Early History of the Town* (*Redditch Indicator* 1887).

Bentley Joseph *Bentley's History, Guide and Directory Worcestershire Vol. I c.1840* (Birmingham).

Bentley Joseph *Bentley's History, Guide and Directory Worcestershire Vol. XII c.1841* (Birmingham).

Birmingham University Field Arch. Unit. *An Arch. Evaluation of land adjacent to Pumphouse Lane 1997* (HWCM 21776).

Birrell Jean ed. *Records of Feckenham Forest Worcestershire c.1236-1377* (Worcestershire Historical Society New Series Volume 21 2006).

Blagrave's Map of Feckenham 1591. Copied 1744 by John Doharty the Younger 1744. Original in The British Library.

Bradford Anne *Royal Enfield: From the Bicycle to the Bullet* (Brewin Books Ltd. 2015).

Census 1851 Tardebigge and Feckenham (Redditch Library).

Coley The Rev. Frederick A. *Centenary 1870-1970 of St. Philip the Apostle Webheath* (Sharp Bros. Printers Evesham 1970).

Dickens Monica *A Thousand Years in Tardebigge* (Cornish Bros. Ltd. 1931).

Eden Sir Frederick *The State of the Poor* originally published 1797. Abridged Edition 1928.

Ellis Maudie *The Squire of Bentley* (Blackwood & Sons 1926).

Feckenham Pauper's Accounts 1836-1843.

Foxall Alan *Old Redditch Pubs* (Warwick Printing Co. Ltd. 2001).

Gaut R.C. *A History of Worcestershire Agriculture* (Littlebury and Co. Ltd. 1939).

Haggard H. Rider *Rural England Vol. I* (Longmans 1906).

A History of the County of Worcester Vol. III - Vol. IV (The Victoria History of the Counties of England. Constable and Co. 1913).

Johnson Mike.

Kelly's Directory Worcestershire 1892, 1928, 1940.

Littlebury's Directory Worcestershire 1873.

Matthew H.C.G. ed. *Oxford Dictionary of National Biography Vol. 24* (Oxford University Press 2004).

Needle District Almanack and Trades Directory for Redditch and Neighbourhood (Various).

Norris Lily *Old Redditch: A Walk Back in Time* (Brewin Books Ltd. 1993).

Population Account 1821 Redditch and Tardebigge (Worcester Record Office BA8552/4 b:850).

Redditch Advertiser 1997.

Redditch Directory 1920, 1963.

Redditch Indicator 1904, 1907, 1908, 1911, 1948, 1995, 2003.

Richardson John *The Local Historian's Encyclopaedia* (Historical Publications 1986).

Tithe Award Map and Apportionment Tardebigge 1838 (Worcester Record Office).

West John *The Administration and Economy of the Forest of Feckenham in the early Middle Ages* (MA University of Birmingham 1964).

Wilks Mick *The Defence of Worcestershire in World War II* (Logaston Press 2007).

Worcestershire Historical Society *Miscellany 1* (WHS 1960 Ebenezer Baylis and Son, Ltd.).

Worcestershire Historical Society NS Vol. 21 *Records of Feckenham Forest c.1236-1377*. Ed. Jean Birrell (Cromwell Press 2006).

Index

INDEX